Breaking into Joy

MEDITATIONS FOR LIVING IN THE LOVE OF CHRIST

Anne Costa

the WORD
among us®
press

Published by The Word Among Us Press
7115 Guilford Drive
Frederick, Maryland 21704
wau.org

18 17 16 15 14   1 2 3 4 5

ISBN: 978-1-59325-260-1
eISBN: 978-1-59325-461-2

Acknowledgments begin on page 215.
Cover design by Koechel Peterson & Associates

Made and printed in the United States of America

Library of Congress Control Number: 2014944076

To my husband, Michael,

and my daughter, Mary, who bring daily joy into

my heart and my life.

Contents

Introduction

In preparation for writing this book, I spent an entire weekend contemplating joy. Now, I can tell you that at the beginning of that weekend, I was not feeling particularly joyful; in fact, I was battling an inner gloominess. I thought, how ironic that I should be writing a book entitled *Breaking into Joy* when I was feeling anything but! God truly does have a sense of humor, doesn't he? Yet I can tell you that by the end of that weekend, I was convinced beyond all doubt of this: that as sure as my life (and yours) will bring times of almost unbearable sorrow and strife, it will also surely bring forth a deep and abiding joy.

How do I know this? Because God says so! His word is filled with promises of joy and examples of how joy reigned in the hearts of his followers against all odds. Still, there may be times when we find it difficult to take God at his word. I know there was a time in my life when I had no idea what joy was or how it could change my life. Joy was as foreign to me as some ancient language spoken across the sea. More than that, it was a language my heart just could not speak, no matter how hard I tried or wished it to be. I was living my life as though I had reached the conclusion that joy was something that was meant for other people and not for me.

Thankfully, the Lord had other plans! Now joy is a constant companion in my life, an old friend. I have received joy as another one of God's most precious gifts, bubble-wrapped in hope and tied with a ribbon of faith. Joy came into my life through an infusion of grace by the Holy Spirit, little by little, one drop at a time. As the years have passed, I can look back now and marvel at how joy has become like a fountain overflowing in my life—even when, like during that weekend, my feelings or mood may have been at an all-time low. Maybe that is how I know for sure that this joy is real, true, authentic, and a direct lifeline from the Lord. You cannot know Jesus and not possess genuine joy. To phrase it another way, to know Jesus is to know joy.

If you are trying to recover or reclaim joy in your life or if you have been seeking it for what seems like your entire life, Jesus and the Holy Spirit will meet you right where you are. They will bring you on a journey, and as you accompany them, it may sometimes feel and look as if you have taken a wrong turn. But hold fast, because just up the road joy will always be waiting for you. Don't be surprised if joy doesn't appear right away because it often takes time to recognize the subtleties of true joy in our lives.

Think of joy as a seashell that has washed upon the shore after a summer storm. You may discover its flash of beauty from a distance, half buried beneath the sand. Just as you may have to dig a little to uncover the shell, you may also have to sift through your feelings and life experiences to find a deeper joy. Just as the magnificent rays of the sun can be seen filtering through the storm clouds, so too can joy break through the sorrows of our lives if we let it happen.

Breaking into Joy was written for you as you travel along your own path toward a deep, abiding joy. These reflections and prayers will help you stay the course as you seek authentic joy, peace, and contentment in your life. It doesn't matter where you are but where you want to be on the road to joy. This book will help you celebrate each step along the way.

Joyfully yours,
Anne Costa

Bearing Fruit

The fruit of the Spirit is . . . joy.

—GALATIANS 5:22

Joy is mentioned almost two hundred and fifty times in Scripture, so it must be an important part of being a Christian. However, you might not know it! How many times have you encountered sour-faced Christians who are quick to judge and slow to smile, and who generally walk around as if they have the weight of the world on their shoulders? I have to admit that I've been one of those Christians at times because I let life's circumstances steal my joy.

Worries, pressures, disappointments, and stress are the weeds that crowd out the fruit of joy in our hearts. If we think of our hearts as gardens, joy is that beautiful, bold sunflower that can grow to towering heights when we are properly tending the soil. Since joy is a fruit of the Holy Spirit, its seed is perpetually planted and waiting to sprout in our hearts. It's up to us to nurture that seed.

To be a good gardener, we have to be willing to get our hands dirty. That means getting to the root of those things that are choking off joy. This takes courage and fortitude. If the roots run deep and the weeds have been around for a long time, we may even need professional help to make room for joy. For example, addiction and joy cannot live in the same garden!

Once we have cleared a place for joy, we have to tend to the holes that are left behind. The best way to fill these holes is through the sacraments. The open spaces in our hearts need to be filled with the presence of God, which we encounter most profoundly in the Eucharist and the Sacrament of Reconciliation. The path to lasting joy is through regular participation in the sacraments.

Finally, a good gardener takes time to admire the beauty that is revealed as a result of his efforts. He lets that beauty seep into his soul so that he can carry it with him wherever he goes. This is the fruit of joy in full bloom, so that regardless of outside conditions, the beauty of joy endures.

Lord, be the Master Gardener of my heart.

Joy Note: How will the fruit of joy blossom in your life today?

Releasing Our Grip

"Do not store up for yourselves treasures on earth."

—Matthew 6:19

Have you ever tried to extricate a toy from the clutched fist of a stubborn toddler? Or wrangle a cell phone from an insolent teenager? Or even attempt to coax the remote from the possession of your beloved spouse? Not easy, is it? All of these instances speak in a small way to the reality that we tend to hold onto things far too tightly and for far too long. The Bible has a word for this: covetousness.

Two of the Ten Commandments warn us directly not to covet, but nearly all of them deal with the consequences of a longing to take possession of things or people and an inappropriate desire for what doesn't belong to us. According to Catholic apologist Fr. Vincent Serpa, OP, "Coveting is an inordinate attachment to things. It is being obsessed with having. To be obsessed with something is to make a god of it."[1] That is a violation of the first commandment, "Thou shall have no other gods before me." An inordinate attachment can also lead us to steal or commit adultery or spend Sunday shopping at the mall instead of going to Mass.

Our society bombards us with the message that the more we have, the happier we will be, and for a short time, that may be true. Yet material things will never bring us the lasting joy our souls are longing for or the fulfillment we seek. Only the intangible and unseen Spirit of God can fill us and complete us. We can't "see" love; we can only "be" love. God's love is truly the most valuable possession we can have. It makes us eternally rich, but we have to let go of our things long enough to receive it.

A wise teacher once advised his student that to "have it all," you must use your riches to make yourself poor. Jesus said a similar thing to a rich young man in his day (Mark 10:17-22). No matter what times we live in, releasing our grip on things will lead us to greater joy.

Lord, help me to let go of all that is keeping me from receiving the treasure of your love.

Joy Note: To what (or whom) are you holding on too tightly?

A Saving Rest

Stand at the crossroads, and look . . .
where the good way lies; and walk in it,
and find rest for your souls.

—Jeremiah 6:16, NRSV

How many of us are rushing around on spiritual life support, just trying to get through another day? For those of us in the Western world, the burden of physical labor has often been removed. Instead, we have mental fatigue and emotional overload. And exhaustion is the archenemy of joy.

Mental and emotional fatigue comes from many sources. We live in a fast-paced, complicated society. Our communication with others can be largely impersonal or functional. We are often faced with layers of bureaucracy that seem to lead us nowhere. This way of living may leave us feeling disconnected, distracted, or deeply wounded.

But the Church in her wisdom has a way of helping us combat this situation. There are built-in rhythms and respites for prayer and recollection right at our fingertips, in the forms of adoration and the Liturgy of the Hours. Adoration is the practice of setting aside holy hours with

Jesus exposed in a monstrance in a chapel or church. All in attendance remain in silence, and it is a time when you can "just be" with Jesus and bask in his presence and love. I have often visited Jesus in this way and have felt as though his living waters of joy were streaming back into my heart from the monstrance as I sat there.

The Liturgy of the Hours or Divine Office is the practice of reciting prayers at set times throughout the day. Most priests and religious and many faithful participate in this ancient form of prayer. It offers a pause in the action whereby we can be renewed in spirit and in joy. These prayers can be found in book form and even on the Internet in an audio version.

We can't change our world or the pace of it, but we can reorder our hearts and priorities. Sometimes we have to do things differently or do different things to bring joy back into our hearts. Our Church provides us with beautiful alternatives to combat the burden of busyness that we carry each day.

Lord, bring rest to my soul!

Joy Note: Have you taken a prayer break today?

What Is Your Witness?

The truthful witness saves lives.

—PROVERBS 14:25

I spent most of my twenties outside the Catholic Church and consequently outside of God's grace. They were troubling years of searching and rebellion not too different from the experience of the younger son in Jesus' parable of the prodigal son. While I was out there dabbling in things that could never bring me peace or put to rest the confusion in my soul, there were certain signs and experiences that stirred a remembrance within me of what I had left behind.

There was one particular sign that acted as a witness and a reminder that the Lord used to bring me back to him. It was the crucifix that I noticed some people wearing around their necks. For me, the crucifix was (and still is) a distinct witness to what Catholicism is all about, and it sets Catholics apart from their brothers and sisters of other Christian traditions, who usually wear a cross without the corpus.

The other sign was the witness of joy that many Catholics displayed. Joy is something you just can't fake, and whenever I encountered a joyful person, it stirred something deep within me. I remember one woman in particular who was always open and accepting of me. She embodied the words of Fr. Henri Nouwen, who wrote in *The Genesee Diary*, "Real joy always wants to share. It belongs to the nature of joy to communicate itself to others and to invite others to take part in the gifts we have received."[2] What a beautiful way to live out our faith!

Most of us don't think of ourselves as witnesses, but we are, and all the time. Only God knows how he will use our presence and willingness to be a witness. But sharing joy will not only help others; it can also increase the joy in our own hearts. You are walking in a truth that others desperately need, and that is a cause of great joy! How will you bear witness to them so that their lives can be changed and their souls can be saved— just like mine was?

Lord, show me the way to be a witness of joy and hope to others.

Joy Note: How will you share your joy today?

One Small Spark

"If any want to become my followers, let them deny themselves."

—MARK 8:34, NRSV

When confronted with the choice between a cupcake and a slice of watermelon, let's face it—most of us will choose the cupcake. However, if we were to turn the choice into a spiritual exercise and engage in a tiny act of self-denial by choosing the watermelon (or going without dessert), we would find ourselves further down the path toward joy. Habitual sacrifice and small acts of self-denial can jump-start joy in our lives, especially when we offer them up for others and out of love for Jesus. Most of us learned this truth in Religion 101 but forget to apply it to our lives on a daily basis.

A small sacrifice is like a heavenly spark in our hearts: the more we do it, the more the light of heaven shines through us here on earth. For most of us, when it comes to sacrifice, the key is "small." Jesus makes this point in the parable of the ten pounds (Luke 19:11-27). After the servant who is given one pound to do business in his master's absence turns it into ten pounds, the master says, "Well done, good servant! You have been faithful in this very small matter; take charge of ten cities" (19:17).

We, too, are called to start out small and grow in our ability to offer sacrifices as we do our spiritual work here on earth. Too often we get discouraged and give up altogether or never even start because we think that we have to engage in grandiose efforts of sacrifice to please Jesus. But this is a trap. It is the measure of love with which we engage in sacrifice that matters. When God says, "I desire mercy, not sacrifice" (cf. Hosea 6:6), he is teaching us that our sacrifices should not be empty gestures or a source of spiritual pride.

In the midst of our affluent, over-the-top culture, a tiny sacrifice can go a long way. We are called to witness in this way to others, who may have never heard the message that going without or giving of ourselves is the swiftest path toward fulfillment and joy.

Father, help me to make small sacrifices with great love.

Joy Note: How have you denied yourself today?

What Is Joy?

"I have told you this so that my joy may be in you and your joy may be complete."

—JOHN 15:11

In the introduction of this book, I mentioned that there was a time when I didn't know what joy was and certainly had never experienced it. I know that there are many more people out there who don't know what joy is or how they can have it in their lives. Are you still looking for joy to break into your life?

Here's what I have learned about joy so far. Joy is the primary characteristic of an obedient heart and the consequence of a submitted soul. Maybe that's why so many people seem to be living joyless lives. Obedience and submission are two concepts that our culture works overtime to submerge under its counterfeit values of hedonism and personal autonomy at all costs.

Nevertheless, joy is 100 percent hands down guaranteed when we follow God's ways and walk in his will. When we obey God and submit ourselves to him, our lives become not only joyful but also victorious. The problem is that we are often looking for joy in all the wrong places.

When we equate joy with ease or the feelings that we get when life goes our way, we reduce it to something as fickle as emotions and subject it to outside circumstances. Two things to remember: joy is an "inside job," and it's not just a good feeling but the completeness and peace we find through living our lives in a state of grace.

Jesus makes joy possible by satisfying the hunger of our hearts and the restlessness of our souls. In fact, Jesus' whole life is a lesson in joy. That's because he walked in perfect obedience to his Father, and he tells us and shows us how to do that too. Every step we take with Jesus leads us closer to the unending joy that flows from God's love.

We will never know the fullness of joy until we get to heaven, but we can come as close as grace allows. Joy is a worthy goal. It requires us to exercise our free will in pursuit and imitation of the excellent life of Christ, in whom our joy will one day be complete.

Lord, lead me to joy.

Joy Note: What is your definition of "joy"?

Praying Your Way

"Lord, teach us to pray."

—LUKE 11:1

"Don't pray when you feel like it. Have an appointment with the Lord and keep it." This sound advice, attributed to the inspirational writer and Holocaust survivor Corrie ten Boom, is for all of us, no matter what our stations or situations in life.

Our prayers don't have to be fancy; they don't even have to make sense! If you are like me, you are probably going to need some grace to keep you from critiquing or censoring your prayers. Try to think of prayer as having a conversation with your best friend. You don't stop to think about what you are saying because you know that anything you say will be understood and accepted. You don't have to worry about offending or being "spiritually correct" with your words; you just pour out your heart. No matter what you are feeling, you can pray with confidence that the Lord is listening with a life-affirming grace that will bring love and power into your circumstance.

Many people suggest that you start your time of prayer with praise, and why not? God doesn't need our praise, but he certainly deserves it, and praise has a way of opening our hearts to God's infinite possibilities. Praise functions to lift our spirits to a higher ground. No matter what our mood or mind-set is before we start to praise, we feel lighter in our spirits as a result, because our hearts were created to praise God. We fulfill our deepest yearnings when we praise.

Some of our most sincere and efficacious prayers can be prayed when we are too tired to pray. They are the ones that we speak with a whisper, when our guard is down or when we are just about to fall asleep. These prayers are short and to the point and give God a chance to have his say. Sometimes a prayer can simply be "Lord, I am open to your word; speak into my heart."

No matter how we pray, however, one thing we can be sure of: when we make an appointment with the Lord for prayer, he will always keep it!

Lord, give me a heart full of prayers and praise!

Joy Note: Have you prayed today?

Believing Is Receiving

"Therefore I tell you, all that you ask for in prayer, believe that you will receive it and it shall be yours."

—MARK 11:24

Are you seeking a breakthrough in your life? Have you been waiting for the course of your life to change or for some release from the status quo? Maybe you are seeking "the next level" in your life, whether that is a deeper intimacy, a better job, or freedom from a particular habit or burden.

The truth is that we can't be alive and not at some point reach that impasse where we are seeking something more. In fact, I believe it is the Lord himself who brings us to the precipice of our own sense of limitation because he wants us to grow, change, and be transformed!

What would happen if you were to act as if you had already received what you've been praying for? I'm not suggesting that you embrace delusion but simply follow the advice of Jesus, who says that we should believe that our prayers have been answered even before we have an outward sign that they have been. Why do you think he said that? What purpose could there be to living in this way?

Jesus is instructing us in the power of faith. Our belief and trust in him have a power and force all their own. Sincere and simple faith is a dynamic, active, and transformative source of grace and change in our lives and in our world.

This is *good news*! We don't have to stay stuck in our ruts. We don't have to put a chain around the desires of our hearts. Faith can break through the barriers, real or artificial, that keep us from our true destinies in Christ Jesus and from the joy he has for us. Just as a candle cannot fulfill its true function until it has been ignited, we will not be everything we are called to be until our hearts are ignited by faith. Faith is the conviction of things not seen (Hebrews 11:1), and breakthroughs, by their very nature, call upon us to look and leap beyond what is to what could be.

Our prayers, when we believe that they have already been answered, are the bridge to the other side of that breakthrough and all that is waiting for us when we get there.

Lord, thank you for answering my prayer!

Joy Note: What answer to prayer have you received?

The Joy of the Lord

The joy of the LORD is your strength.
—NEHEMIAH 8:10, NRSV

If you are looking for a "mantra" to meditate on or a prayer to pray, here is a powerful one: "The joy of the LORD is my strength." It is adapted from the verse above from the Book of Nehemiah. Nehemiah's story is an interesting one. He was not just a spiritual leader and prophet during a very difficult time in the lives of the Israelites. He also had a difficult and dangerous job: he was a cupbearer for the emperor, Artaxerxes.

A cupbearer was someone who tasted the contents of whatever the emperor drank to assure that it wasn't poisoned. Imagine what a bad day at work would have been like for Nehemiah! It's no wonder that he needed strength. But that is not all the Lord gave Nehemiah. He was also given courage and wisdom and, thankfully, a new job, at his behest, as governor of Jerusalem.

Nehemiah asked to return to Jerusalem at a time when the city was in ruins and poverty. The exiled Israelites had returned to a city that was destroyed and in chaos. Nehemiah provided strong leadership and encouraged the people by his example. As a result, Jerusalem prospered, and its walls were rebuilt. Through it all, Nehemiah reminded the people where their strength lay.

"The joy of the LORD is your strength" was an admonition to the Israelites to stop grieving over their losses and to turn away from their bitterness and sadness to "make great rejoicing" (Nehemiah 8:12, NRSV). Just like the returning exiles, we, too, need to be reminded to stop lamenting over what is wrong and proclaim what is good and hopeful in our world today. Our strength still comes from joy, not from complaining and focusing on what is wrong.

It's a huge temptation of our times to dwell on the negative. We are so aware of what is wrong with our culture and society that we fail to see what is right. When we perpetually point out the worst, we lose our hope and our spiritual strength to make things better. Remember that as God's joy is available to us at every moment, we can and will move those mountains of negativity and rebuild the ruins around us.

Lord, your joy is my strength!

Joy Note: Will you taste the cup of his joy today?

You Get What You Give

"Give and gifts will be given to you; a good measure, packed together, shaken down, and overflowing, will be poured into your lap. For the measure with which you measure will in return be measured out to you."

—LUKE 6:38

The great preacher and writer Norman Vincent Peale wrote, "Joy increases as you give it." It's such a simple concept, one that follows the law of reciprocity and the words of Jesus from the Gospel of St. Luke. The beautiful truth is that when we give away the goodness and gifts that we have been given, we receive them back in an even greater portion. This is "God's economy."

Think of joy as an infectious giggle. Maybe you're in an important meeting or at church, and something strikes you as very funny. You start to giggle, and no matter how hard you try to contain it, it spills out, and when it does, it starts to affect those around you. They start to giggle, even when they don't know what was so funny in the first place. When they join in, you start to giggle all the more! When joy spreads in this way, we can be sure to receive it back.

There's a woman from my town who goes by the name of "Joygerm Joan." She has dedicated her entire adult life to spreading joy and has even formed a ministry dedicated to joy. Each year there is a parade or event for all of the "Joygerms" from our community and beyond to come together and celebrate. It's a public demonstration of joy in action, and it's always great fun.

The last Joygerm gathering I attended took place in the middle of the biggest shopping mall in our area. We were a sight to behold: "Red Hat" ladies, several clowns, a chorus of children and bell ringers, some rescued greyhounds and their owners, and a man with an accordion, along with everyday folks from all walks of life, singing, laughing, and spreading joy. Before we knew it, we were circled by curious shoppers who couldn't resist the infectious spirit in their midst. What had started out as a small contingent ended up with hundreds of people sharing an afternoon of fun, frolic, and joy—a good measure, pressed down, shaken together, and running over!

Lord, make me an instrument of your joy!

Joy Note: How can you be a "Joygerm" today?

If Joy Were a Color

*Therefore, encourage one another and
build one another up.*

—1 Thessalonians 5:11

If joy were a color, what would it be? That's the title of
a poem I wrote many years ago. It was inspired by my
friend Krista. She was a true friend who always challenged me to live with a childlike spirit and to find something to delight in every day.

That whimsical poem became a mission for us as we
went about asking others which color they would ascribe
to "joy." As you might imagine, each person had his or
her own idea. Some said green because it's the color of
nature; others chose pink, and I favored yellow. It was
fun to hear them explain why they had chosen a certain
color as they shared their individual stories of joy. It still
brings a smile to my heart when I think of that poem.

It's a reminder that we all need to help each other
recall times of joy in our lives. This is how we can
encourage one another and build one another up, as
St. Paul says in the Scripture verse above. It could even
become a personal ministry for us to help others conjure up memories of delight to lighten their spirits. After

all, we all know that life can be hard sometimes, or even just mundane.

One of the best places to bring a ministry of joy and encouragement is to a nursing home or senior center. These places are bursting with the potential for joy as people who have lived long and fruitful lives are invited to share their stories and memories with others. Even when people experience dementia, they are often still able to remember times of joy in their lives.

Words are a powerful way to connect with one another; we can use them to build up or tear down, bring delight or deep despair. The more we encourage one another, the more encouraged we become! It just works that way. There's always room for more joy in our days. Let it be your mission to bring more of it to others today.

Lord, lift me up so that I can experience delight and bring encouragement to others who need it.

Joy Note: If joy were a color, what would it be?

A Father's Sign

He will shelter you with his pinions,
and under his wings you may take refuge.

—PSALM 91:4

Do you know what "pinions" are? I didn't until I looked it up as I was reading this verse, which is one of my favorites. Pinions are feathers, and when I discovered this, I was reminded of something that makes this verse even more meaningful to me. Here's the story.

After my father died, I felt vulnerable in the world. He was my mentor and my hero. No matter what problem I brought to him, he always seemed to have the right answer. His gentle encouragement was always there for me; his counsel was forever wise.

Two years after his death, I went through a particularly difficult period in my life. My work life was stressful, and I was caring for my mother, who was failing in health and memory. The sheer weight of my troubles was wearing my faith thin, and I was feeling far away from God. One night, out of desperation, I prayed for a sign that my father was near. I needed to know that he was in heaven, still watching out for me. Determined to know, I specifically asked for that sign to be a feather.

The next day I was preoccupied, as usual, as I crossed the street to enter my office. Stepping onto the curb, I glanced down and noticed something sticking straight up from a crack in the sidewalk. You guessed it—it was a single white feather! A skeptic might call it a coincidence, but since then, this same sign has appeared many times, bringing me a great and renewed sense of joy in my heart each time.

We should never hesitate to ask God or any one of the communion of saints for a sign when we need it most. I'm convinced that they are ready, willing, and able to share the joy of heaven with us, one little sign at a time.

Lord, thank you for the little ways you open heaven to bring us your signs of joy!

Joy Note: Do you need a sign today?

Buried Treasure

"The kingdom of heaven is like a treasure buried in a field."

—Matthew 13:44

Tucked in the back corner of my jewelry drawer is a tiny box. It's a gift I received from my daughter one Christmas when she was four or five. It contains a collection of everything that was precious to her at the time: a gold ring from a bubble-gum machine, a dollar-store pearl necklace, a smooth pink stone, a ghost pin from Halloween, and a tiny bottle of blue nail polish. Every time I open that box, my heart melts as I remember her innocence and reflect upon the gift that she has been in my life.

Sometimes joy is like that tiny box. Even though joy is a precious gift that God wants to give us, it sometimes gets pushed back to some remote corner of our hearts by all the clutter and chaos of our lives, and we forget that it's there. We can become so busy that we don't take notice of the tiny (and not so tiny) treasures that each day brings.

Here's one example from my own life. No matter what time I get up in the morning on workdays, it seems that I am always rushing. Maybe it's the adrenaline, maybe it's the stress, but by the time I am halfway through my morning commute, I'm racing down the highway at warp speed. Every now and again, though, the Holy Spirit gets my attention and invites me to look up. When I do, I am often met with a glorious sunrise—an expanse of sky painted in pinks and golds that takes my breath away. And in that moment, I have unwrapped the gift of God's joy.

Did you know that repeatedly refusing to accept God's joy can lead us to "acedia" or spiritual sloth? According to the *Catechism of the Catholic Church,* acedia is a sin against God's love, to "refuse the joy that comes from God . . . and to be repelled by divine goodness" (2094). I hope that you never experience acedia because a life without joy is a life without God. It is up to us to dig deeply in our lives to discover the buried treasure of God's gift of joy.

Lord, help me to uncover the treasure of your joy.

Joy Note: How will you open God's gift of joy today?

A Special Remedy

They that hope in the LORD *will renew their strength.*

—ISAIAH 40:31

"Just a spoonful of sugar helps the medicine go down." For years after viewing the movie *Mary Poppins*, I insisted that my father give me a teaspoon of sugar mixed with water with every pill or medication I had to take. Somehow it always helped, and the memory still makes me smile of his patient response to my demand for "shugy water." As I grew and so did my problems, he would often provide me with some wise counsel and ask with a wink, "Would you like some sugar water to go along with that?"

Today I ask my heavenly Father to sweeten the rough spots and help me to swallow the "bitter pills" of life. He never runs out of patience in responding to my requests. He might not eliminate a sickness or difficult circumstance; after all, it may ultimately bring me his healing medicine and greater spiritual health. But he *will* give me a teaspoonful of hope to keep me going and renew my strength along the way. In essence, hope is God's sugar water for our souls.

According to the Book of Proverbs, "Hope deferred makes the heart sick" (13:12), so we need to do everything we can to hold onto hope. One thing we can do is to pray specifically for hope by simply reciting, "Jesus, I hope in you." Or we can pray the Church's traditional Act of Hope, which follows:

O my God, relying on Your almighty power and infinite mercy and promises, I hope to obtain pardon of my sins, the help of Your grace and life everlasting, through the merits of Jesus Christ, my Lord and Redeemer. Amen.

Another suggestion is to personalize the Scripture verse from Romans 15:13 in this way:

May the God of hope fill me with all joy and peace in believing, so that I may abound in hope by the power of the Holy Spirit.

Whichever prayer you choose, a daily dose of hope will see you through.

Lord, thank you for the sweet remedy of hope.

Joy Note: Have you taken your medicine today?

A Blank Slate

The steadfast love of the LORD never ceases,
his mercies never come to an end;
they are new every morning.

—LAMENTATIONS 3:22-23, NRSV

Sheila is a self-taught artist. Her paintings are so beautiful that you would never guess that she has no formal training. Every brushstroke expresses her great love of all living things and her thrill of capturing the God-given beauty in the people and places that she depicts on canvas. One day I asked her to describe the greatest joy that she experiences through painting.

Her answer surprised me: the greatest joy she feels is when she is looking at the blank canvas, even before she picks up the brush. It is then that she is filled with a holy sense of exhilaration and awe that comes from cooperating with an inspiration that is greater than she is. In those moments of surrender, before she commits her vision to canvas, she is filled with absolute joy.

In a spiritual sense, God's infinite love gives us the chance to experience the blessings of a similar blank slate. This happened to my friend Lana. She was having a difficult time coping with how her life had unfolded.

After a series of personal losses that included the death of a friend and estrangement from her family, she felt defeated and alone. Full of regrets, she cried out to the Lord for his mercy and a sense of direction. Her prayer was "Lord, help me out of this mess!" Almost immediately, the Lord spoke to her heart with this phrase: "I can make masterpieces out of your mud pies."

For Lana, it was a profound revelation that God can turn our messes into masterpieces by giving us a new canvas and a clean slate each day. He can take our mistakes and bring forth great beauty when we let him. His mercies make possible a new creation and a new direction for our lives. If God can do that for Lana, he can surely do that for you and me—and that is something that can truly inspire us with joy.

Heavenly Father, I am grateful for your brand-new mercies every day.

Joy Note: Will you surrender your "mud pies" to God today? What masterpiece will you create together?

Consider It All Joy

Consider it all joy, my brothers, when you encounter various trials, for you know that the testing of your faith produces perseverance. And let perseverance be perfect, so that you may be perfect and complete, lacking in nothing.

—James 1:2-4

When you think about it, God's love, by necessity, must be a refining love. That's because his love is perfectly pure, and our souls are in need of that purity, like flowers in need of rain. God's love is a transforming love that molds, shapes, and reshapes us lovingly into the people we are called to be. Most often those changes and refining times are painful, difficult, and confusing.

Blessedly, refining times don't last forever. They have a purpose: to bring forth greater beauty, joy, and peace in our lives. When we look back, we often recognize them as the most important moments in our lives. My friend Kathy was diagnosed with leukemia and spent more than a year enduring a grueling regime of chemotherapy to save her life. During those months, she took the opportunity not only to surrender her physical well-being to God, but to seek healing for her mind, emotions, past hurts, and present spiritual state.

Submitting herself in this way to God's refining love was an active choice to trust God as she faced some of the scariest moments of her life. Because she did, one of her most intense trials ended up being one of the most gifted and grace-filled periods of her life. She didn't waste a single day of her sickness as she offered up her sufferings for the causes of others. As a result, she can recount many blessings from that time of testing and has since used her experiences to encourage and accompany others facing the same difficult journey.

This is the beauty and blessing of our trials and the cause of our joy. Our perseverance is brought to perfection when we can use our past or present painful situations to help others. It's a beautiful circle of sacrifice that enriches even the most sorrowful of circumstances. Our lives will take on new meaning and depth when we consider it all joy to be completed by our Father's refining and perfect love.

Lord, give me the grace to receive your refining love.

Joy Note: What sacrifice can you offer up for others today?

Heart Health

With all vigilance guard your heart,
for in it are the sources of life.

—PROVERBS 4:23

This verse from Proverbs is a powerful reminder of one of the most important responsibilities we have as followers of Christ: to guard our hearts. We are called to do so on a physical, emotional, and spiritual level because the heart is the source of life for each of us. Since our bodies are the temples of the Holy Spirit (1 Corinthians 6:19), tending to our "heart health" becomes not only a physical but also a spiritual exercise.

According to the *Catechism of the Catholic Church*, our hearts are also the spiritual center of our beings:

The heart is our hidden center, beyond the grasp of our reason and of others; only the Spirit of God can fathom the human heart and know it fully. The heart is the place of decision, deeper than our psychic drives. It is the place of truth, where we choose life or death. It is the place of encounter, because as image of God we live in relation: it is the place of covenant. (2563)

As beautiful as that description is, Scripture also reminds us that out of the heart come "evil thoughts, murder, adultery, unchastity, theft, false witness, [and] blasphemy" (Matthew 15:19). When we give our hearts over to sin in this way, they become hardened. That is why we have to guard them and cooperate with God's grace so that he can give us a new heart and a new spirit, removing from our bodies a heart of stone and giving us a heart of flesh (Ezekiel 36:26).

How do we go about guarding our hearts? There has never been a more tender heart than the immaculate heart of our Blessed Mother. We are told more than once in Scripture that she kept all things and pondered them in her heart (Luke 2:19, 51). While she was without sin, she was not without sorrow. But although she experienced sorrow, as we do, her heart was a beautiful garden of grace. One way that we can guard our hearts is to learn how to ponder as Mary did. Listening to that "still small voice" within us (cf. 1 Kings 19:12) will help us avoid any evil intentions and to embrace joy.

Lord, show me the way to ponder all things in my heart as Mary did.

Joy Note: How will you guard your heart today?

God's Glue

The sacrifice acceptable to God is a broken spirit;
a broken and contrite heart, O God, you will not despise.
—PSALM 51:17, NRSV

The Nobel Prize winning playwright Eugene O'Neill is credited with the following saying: "Man is born broken; he lives by mending. The grace of God is glue." O'Neill lived a very troubled life; he was plagued with alcoholism and depression and suffered the estrangement and suicides of his two sons. But I can't help thinking that this saying, filled with hope, flows from the seven years that he spent in a Catholic boarding school as a youth.

It was during those years that he began writing to express or perhaps to suppress the inner anguish that was already beginning to brew in his soul. In spite of tremendous personal misery, he kept going. His saying is a reminder that God provides his glue for all of us to cope with our brokenness.

We miss a tremendous opportunity to come to know God in a deeper way when we try to deny that we are broken. Our quests for perfection and outward appearances of strength and total "togetherness" are not what God desires from us. Sometimes it is hard to believe this truth because in this life, we can experience rejection, ridicule, or shame when we don't "measure up" or meet every challenge with success. These experiences lead us to hide or cover up the broken pieces within us.

Yet God urges us and, in fact, is inviting us to offer our brokenness as a sacrifice so that he can take our broken hearts and failed attempts and mend them with his loving and patient hands. If we live by his mending, then we will come to know the true joy that flows from God's glue because his grace will make us whole.

When we are broken, it is hard for us to envision what that wholeness will look like. But God has his vision of perfection for us tucked within his heart. He sees the restored version of us after his glue has been applied, and it is greater than we can ever imagine. Offer your brokenness to him, and trust that his mending will bring you joy.

Lord, mend me with your grace.

Joy Note: Have you offered your brokenness to God today?

Turning the Tide

Though the Lord may give you the bread of adversity
and the water of affliction, . . . when you turn to the right
or when you turn to the left, your ears shall hear a word
behind you, saying, "This is the way; walk in it."

—Isaiah 30:20, 21, NRSV

As I was writing this book, a disturbed young man opened fire in an elementary school just days before Christmas in Newtown, Connecticut, killing twenty schoolchildren, six administrators, his mother, and himself. The tragedy brought unfathomable sorrow to that little town, the entire nation, and beyond.

As word spread of the horrific event, the streets of Newtown began to fill with anguished parents, frightened neighbors, and a steady stream of first responders and news reporters. Hour by hour, as the awful extent of the loss began to sink in, people headed toward the open doors of every church in town. One woman who was interviewed said, "We are going to be living at our church until we can come to some sense of peace about what has just happened here."

She was referring to St. Rose of Lima Church in Newtown, where many of the youngest victims attended and eight of the children's funerals were held. I spoke with the church secretary about a month after the tragedy and was told that they had received more than one hundred thousand packages and letters from well-wishers from around the world. She assured me that each item would be "opened with great reverence in thanksgiving for the gifts and kind words received."

Another amazing outpouring of love occurred during the weeks after the tragedy as people engaged in twenty-six random acts of kindness in memory of the twenty-six who had died. There were reports from around the country of such acts of kindness, from people leaving a bag of groceries on a neighbor's doorstep to paying off a lay-away bill for a stranger. These small gestures helped us all turn against the tide of evil, step beyond our pain, and walk in the way of the Lord to bring a measure of joy out of unspeakable sorrow. It is comforting to know that no matter what happens, we always have that choice.

Lord, help me to heed your word and walk in your ways.

Joy Note: Have you offered a random act of kindness lately?

Catch the Vision

Whatever is true, whatever is honorable,
whatever is just, whatever is pure, whatever is lovely,
whatever is gracious, if there is any excellence and if there
is anything worthy of praise, think about these things.

—PHILIPPIANS 4:8

Lovers of opera get lost in the nuances of sight, sound, and story that come together in a sublime experience of the senses. Those with an artistic eye can discern a depth of emotion that others can't begin to see from a one-dimensional canvas. As Christians, we are created with a fine-tuned spirit that is drawn to the things of God. The greater our love for God, the more we will be able to recognize and appreciate all that is contained in the verse above from Philippians.

It's no secret that the world dwells in the negative and seems to be constantly spiraling down slippery slopes toward spiritual, moral, and cultural decay. Yet if every Christian heeded the call of this verse, I believe that we could change the world in no time. If we let our hearts get caught up in the grandeur of God's righteousness, we could shift the trajectory of our culture and bring about a spiritual renaissance hitherto unseen in our world. Do you have a vision for that? Can you see it happening?

Prayer will get us there, coupled with a firm desire to discipline our thoughts to dwell only on that which is excellent. Practicing this habit in our daily lives will cause not just a mighty shift in our own minds and hearts; it will also have a ripple effect that will touch everyone around us. Before we know it, we will have a revolution of grace that can't be contained! It will be like a wildfire, ignited by the Holy Spirit of God.

We often call upon the Holy Spirit to "renew the face of the earth." But the only way that he can do it is through you and me. We have to make it our goal, our vision, and our hope. We have to be willing to throw down our negativity, apathy, and cynicism. Instead, we must take up the causes of nobility, honor, truth, purity, and righteousness, because our spirits were made for such things as these.

Lord, use me to bring about a revolution of your righteousness to renew the face of the earth.

Joy Note: What are you waiting for?

First Things First

You shall love the Lord your God with all your heart,
with all your soul, with all your mind,
and with all your strength.

—MARK 12:30

In her autobiography, St. Thérèse of Lisieux proclaimed, "At last I have found it. . . . *MY VOCATION IS LOVE!*"[3] It brought her lifelong joy to embrace this call for her life, which is every Christian's call. She carried out her vocation as a little one of God, childlike and trusting, with a soul that was completely ablaze with love.

Like St. Thérèse, we, too, must discover our unique vocation of love. The first commandment to love God with all of our heart, mind, and strength is the essential ingredient for a good life here and the way to eternal joy in the next. So how do we love in this way? Even though our human love can't compare to God's love, he is not asking us to do the impossible. He is inviting us to a greater surrender and trust in his perfect love so that we might share in it.

When we love with all our hearts, it means that we are able to detach our hearts from anything contrary to

Jesus. Is there any hold on your heart that is crowding out Jesus and your love for him? When we love with all our minds, we submit our intellect and reasoning to God's enlightenment and his Holy Spirit. Then we are able to discern with wisdom how to apply love to life's most difficult situations. What evidence do you have that you love God with your mind? When we love with all our strength, we put all our effort into service and sacrifice. We make it a priority to please God with our actions, and we do this out of love for God, not to save ourselves. In essence, when we love in this way, we love God's ways more than our own.

When there is a disconnect between what God wants and what we hold dear (which are usually our opinions, desires, and ways of doing things), then we know there is room for a deeper love in our hearts. God has always made it clear what he wants. Do you love him enough to want that too?

God, give me the grace to love you with everything that I have.

Joy Note: Do you know what God wants?

The Spiritual Side of Success

*Test yourselves. Do you not realize that
Jesus Christ is in you?*

—2 CORINTHIANS 13:5

I have a confession to make: everything that I have ever
succeeded at in life, I faked first. In fact, everything I have
mastered, from public speaking to managing people to
writing books and being a parent, I have started out by
not having a clue of what I was doing!

It all began when a supervisor suggested that I present a daylong workshop for the staff of the agency where
I was working. I looked at her with stark terror in my
eyes and told her with a trembling voice, "I don't know
how to do that!" And she replied, "You will when you
get done!"

Since then, I have spent my life setting goals that
are just a bit beyond my capabilities. Whether the gap
between what I think I can do and what I set my mind
to do is narrow or wide, I have learned that I can count
on the Lord to be there in that gap—and that is the spiritual side of success. Jesus calls us out of the boat all of the
time. He invites us to face our fears and hand over our
limitations and weaknesses because his "power is made

perfect in weakness" (2 Corinthians 12:9). Fear is the number one faith crusher and a tool that the devil uses to keep us from reaching our potential. Safety has never been the hallmark of a Christian life. Walking by faith requires us to take risks while keeping our eyes on Jesus.

I am not suggesting that you act in an imprudent or dishonest manner, but I am inviting you to stretch yourself beyond your current limits. I am asking you to question those limits and discern if they are self-imposed, a sign of laziness, or a surrender to fear. Take those questions to prayer, asking the Holy Spirit for enlightenment. It's time to get out of the wading pool of life and make your way to the deep end. You don't know how, you say? Well, you will once you get there!

Lord, give me the courage to go beyond my comfort zone and walk in the spirit of success in my life.

Joy Note: What will you do that you cannot do today?

Sing for Joy

The time of singing has come.
—SONG OF SONGS 2:12, NRSV

Fr. Phil has introduced a new ending for some of his homilies. He invites the members of his congregation to join him in singing a rendition of "Rejoice in the Lord always, again I say rejoice!" (cf. Philippians 4:4). It's an upbeat tune that can be sung in a round, and it can't help but lift the spirits of those who sing it. However, I am always amazed at how many people resist the opportunity and sit there stony-faced, refusing to sing. Perhaps they are self-conscious or maybe they think it is silly or improper, but I think the benefits of joining in far outweigh the risks!

Scientists are now confirming what our souls have known all along—that singing is good for our health. Studies show that singing boosts the immune system, improves mood, and even prolongs life.[4] When teachers want to teach new concepts to young children, they will often introduce a song to help them memorize. This works for adults as well.

Singing has always been a part of worshipping God, and many saints are associated with singing. St. Cecilia is the patron saint of singers and musicians because, according to the fifth-century *Acta* that tells of the events of her life, "While the profane music of her wedding was heard, Cecilia was singing in her heart a hymn of love for Jesus, her true spouse." And, of course, King David wrote the psalms and sang many songs to praise God and express his sorrow. Though David was a great warrior and grew to be a spiritual giant, it is thought that he struggled with depression. One way that he may have coped with his dark feelings was to sing.

I don't know of any better way to raise one's spirits than to put on some praise music and join in. St. Augustine said that to sing was to pray twice. Our souls are nourished by the beauty of music and the melodies that capture our hearts. By God's grace, we will all one day join in the celestial choir, offering our praise and adoration to him. But for now, let's not resist the chance to sing for joy.

Jesus, I will offer you a song of joy in thanksgiving for all that you are.

Joy Note: What song will you sing today?

Growing Our Gifts

*I remind you to rekindle the gift of God that
is within you.*

—2 TIMOTHY 1:6, NRSV

"It's never too late to become who you could have been." I love that phrase because it's so true! One of my dearest friends participated in her first musical, *Jesus Christ Superstar*, at the age of sixty-four. She played the Blessed Mother, and it had a profound effect on her spiritual life. Another friend raised six children, worked as a nurse, and at the age of forty, went to law school. When she was fifty-nine, she ran for a seat in the U.S. Congress and won!

The expression of our gifts is ultimately in our hands. They are always present within us, waiting to be cultivated and shared. Likewise, age is not a factor in how we share our talents. Talents are like the bloom of the flower; the potential is always there, but the conditions need to be just right. Some conditions that are right for our gifts and talents to bloom are (1) a healthy dose of enthusiasm and passion; (2) a "gag order" on self-criticism and critique; (3) plenty of rest (energy is required);

(4) regular solitude for time to think, dream, and pray; and (5) a "ritual" of openness to the Holy Spirit.

The last condition is your personal pledge to receive inspiration and direction from the Holy Spirit. Your ritual could be going to Confession, Mass, or Eucharistic adoration. It could be a walk in the woods, an invocation prayer to the Holy Spirit, attending a prayer group, or journaling. Inspiration from the Holy Spirit is like a babbling brook. It is always flowing in the background of our lives. We need to "dip our toe in" and then offer our gifts back to God.

It may be that God will rekindle our gifts in a whole new way. We might discover different, never-before-conceived-of gifts, or we might recover talents that we have long since buried. Joy comes when we let ourselves get caught up and delight in the fact that with God, anything is possible. Our earthly lives are brief in comparison to the eternity that we are invited to spend with Jesus in heaven. So it's never too late to become who God calls us to be.

Lord, rekindle your gifts in me for your glory.

Joy Note: Who could you have been?

A Parting Gift

I will ask the Father, and he will give you another
Advocate to be with you always, the Spirit of truth.

—JOHN 14:16-17

When Jackie dropped off her only child at college for the first time, she admits that it felt like the end of the world. She was overcome with emotion as she thought back on all the years that had flown by, landing them at this bittersweet moment marking the end of her daughter's childhood. As she and her husband drove away from the campus, Jackie surrendered to a torrent of tears that flowed from a heavy heart.

Many mothers and fathers can relate to this scene. The overwhelming feelings of pride, joy, love, and sorrow, all mixed together, are the hallmarks of one of the strongest bonds we experience in life: that of parent and child. A mother and father give everything they have for that moment when they say good-bye to their child so that he or she can become the adult they are called to be.

Do you know that Jesus understands and experienced those exact same emotions, probably in an even deeper way? He, too, after giving all of himself for those he loved, had to leave us. But before he did, he shared a final meal with his disciples and friends and poured out his heart to them, promising that he "[would] not leave [them] orphans" by sending a Comforter, Advocate, and Friend: the Holy Spirit (John 14:18). What an awesome going-away present!

The Holy Spirit is known by many names, but one of the most unique is "the oil of gladness." According to Pope Benedict XVI, "The oil of gladness is the Holy Spirit himself, who was poured out upon Jesus Christ. The Holy Spirit is the gladness that comes from God."[5] So in essence, when God gave us the Holy Spirit, he gave us joy in the form of a Person to be with us always.

Our lives will be touched by tearful good-byes and tremendous triumphs alike. Isn't it a comfort to know that we can call upon the Holy Spirit to anoint us with the oil of gladness to see us through?

Come, Holy Spirit, and be my joy.

Joy Note: How can you bring the oil of joy into the world today?

Our Unchanging Truth

Jesus Christ is the same yesterday, today, and forever.

—Hebrews 13:8

Have you heard the notion that the Catholic Church is hopelessly out of touch with the modern world? Truly there are pressures from all sides, including from within the Church itself, to "get with the times." And while our understanding of Church doctrine unfolds over time, it does so slowly and only through the inspiration and guidance of the Holy Spirit. This process of discernment is necessarily painstaking and slow, especially in comparison with our rapid-fire, ever-changing world.

When I came back to the Church after a long time away, I wasn't sure if I could follow every teaching and I had some "problems" with what the Church taught on several sensitive subjects. I was concerned that the Church might be a little out of touch with life, and I still needed to be convinced that what the Church taught was *right*. So I went about reading everything that I could about the Church's teachings. In my search, I found that the *Catechism, of the Catholic Church* made things especially clear and concise without being burdensome.

I was surprised by the clarity of all that I was learning. I couldn't find anything that didn't make sense! Not only that, but I found that my heart was beginning to be filled with a desire to fully live and embrace the truths that I was coming to understand. In that way, the Truth, who is Jesus, was moving from my head to my heart, and all my preconceived notions and fears were falling away. What I thought was going to be a "tough road to hoe" in obedience became a joy and a journey toward spiritual freedom that continues today.

The world is full of fads and crazes that claim to make life and religion easier, more entertaining, or simply like everyone else's. Yet our Catholic faith, from its founding days, has been countercultural. Our unchanging Savior is our guide, and it's good to remember that where our faith is concerned, keeping up with the times might just be the last thing we want to do.

Lord, I love your unchanging ways.

Joy Note: What unchanging truth brings you the greatest joy?

Behold the Heart

See what love the Father has bestowed on us
that we may be called the children of God.

—1 JOHN 3:1

Tim grew up in a highly competitive family. He and his four brothers all played sports, and they each tried to outdo one another in every game they played. Now grown and with a family of his own, Tim realizes that he and his brothers were not so much competing with each other but for the love and affection of their father. Their father, a retired Army colonel, was somewhat unapproachable and hard to please. Tim always felt that he had to be the best in order to make a positive impression on or even to catch the attention of his dad.

Many of us have had similar upbringings, vying for the limited love and attention of our parents. As the late Christian writer and pastor A. W. Tozer once said, "An infinite God can give all of Himself to each of His children. He does not distribute Himself that each may have a part, but to each one He gives all of Himself as fully as if there were no others."[6]

One translation of 1 John 3:1 states, " See what great love the Father has lavished on us" (NIV), and that word "lavish" is an accurate description of how God loves us. Simply put, there is no limit to God's love for us. The Sacred Heart of Jesus devotion is one way we can try to comprehend God's love. Jesus appeared to St. Margaret Mary Alacoque with a burning heart, full of desire that each of us would "behold the heart that has loved men so much."

It is such a relief to know that we do not have to compete for God's love—and what joy it can bring us! His heart is overflowing for each one of us in a personal and intimate way. We have his full attention all of the time. It's hard to believe that a God who created everything in the universe is likewise interested in every minor detail of our lives, but it's true. Jesus tells us, "Even all the hairs of your head are counted" (Matthew 10:30). Letting go of our tendencies to compare ourselves with others or compete with them will free us up to simply receive God's lavish love.

Thank you, Father for your undivided attention and love.

Joy Note: How will you behold the heart of Jesus today?

A Blessing or a Curse?

*For every kind of beast and bird, of reptile
and sea creature, can be tamed and has been tamed
by the human species, but no human being
can tame the tongue.*

—JAMES 3:7-8

I have adopted the practice that every time I bless myself with holy water, I also make the Sign of the Cross on my lips. It's an important and necessary ritual because if I am going to get into trouble, it will be my mouth that leads the way! While there are times when God uses my words to bring great blessings upon others, there have also been countless times when my tongue has run wild and rampant, causing pain to others and bringing them harm.

The Letter of James likens the human tongue to a fire (3:6). Jesus reminds us that "from the fullness of the heart the mouth speaks" and that on the day of judgment, we will render an account for every careless word we speak (Matthew 12:34, 36)! So if we can know the true condition of our hearts by what comes out of our mouths, we had better pay attention. If our conversations are full of negativity, then we know our hearts need an infusion of joy. If our words are full of jealousy, then we need the grace of humility. Taking a day or week to examine our conversations (with ourselves and others) can reveal a great deal about where we are spiritually and how we might need to pray.

What if we all committed to taming our tongues and using them to encourage others instead of finding fault with them? We could be like my neighbor Jeanne, who strives to find a way to offer a sincere compliment to everyone she converses with throughout her day. It doesn't matter whether she is talking to her boss or the gas station attendant; she looks for a way to encourage and lift that person up. She will be the first to say that this practice requires discipline, especially on days when she is tired or grumpy. But even then, she gets just as much out of it as she gives. The joy in her heart increases by the joy that she brings to others.

Lord, tame my tongue!

Joy Note: How will you use your tongue to bring blessings to others today?

Rejoice Always!

Rejoice in the Lord always. I shall say it again: rejoice!

—PHILIPPIANS 4:4

When Karen's husband left her, the last thing on her mind and heart was joy. She continued going to church but found herself even more resentful when she left. She felt so alone in her misery while those around her seemed to be content, even joyful. She wondered if she would ever feel good again.

By God's grace, Karen kept going to church and receiving the sacraments, in spite of her sadness. She kept her heart open and asked the Lord to restore her joy. One day while entering the adoration chapel, Karen spotted a book on the shelf that caught her eye: *Rejoice in the Lord Always!* by Fr. George Kosicki. Karen felt certain that she was supposed to read that book!

On the first few pages, Karen found the answer to her prayers. It was an explanation of the difference between "rejoicing" and being "joyful."

We are commanded to "rejoice always," but we are not commanded to be always joyful. . . . Rejoicing is something that we can always do—whether in sadness or in joy, whether in darkness or in light. We *don't need to feel joy in order to rejoice.*[7] (emphasis added)

What a relief it was for Karen to discover that rejoicing runs deeper than any fleeting or painful emotion! Instead, rejoicing is releasing our emotions to God in a sacrifice of praise. God is always worthy of our praise, no matter what is going on in our lives because, as Fr. Kosicki reminds us, "To rejoice is to respond to God because he is God."[8] Our souls are made to rejoice, even in sorrow!

There is no one who embodies this paradox more in Scripture than Job. After he learned that he had lost most of his possessions and all of his children, Job "arose and tore his cloak and cut off his hair. He fell to the ground and worshiped. He said, . . . 'Blessed be the name of the LORD!'" (Job 1:20, 21). And like Job, Karen found that God rewarded her in her willingness to rejoice in spite of her circumstance.

Lord, I worship you and give you thanks, no matter how I feel.

Joy Note: Are you rejoicing today?

A Year in a Life

The LORD will guide you always.

—ISAIAH 58:11

Have you ever taken a look at your calendar and wanted to run in the opposite direction? Does the sheer volume of activities and responsibilities inspire you to simply want to go back to bed? I have to admit that this happens to me on a regular basis, but never so much as in this year that I am writing this book.

Without going into too much detail, let me say that this year has been the fullest and most chaotic I have ever experienced. It has been marked by many new and challenging projects at work and at home, some with virtually impossible deadlines that have required superhuman stamina to keep me on track. Before it all began, a co-worker gave me a simple Christmas gift that has become a lifeline in the torrential onslaught that has become my life: a mug with the Scripture verse above from Isaiah 58:11. The full verse goes like this:

> Then the LORD will guide you always
> and satisfy your thirst in parched places,
> will give strength to your bones

And you shall be like a watered garden,
  like a flowing spring whose waters never fail.

When I received the mug, I knew immediately that I would be clinging to this Scripture verse to get me through this year. I also felt that God was speaking his peace directly into my heart and life with these encouraging words. And guess what? He has.

As I am writing this reflection, three-quarters of the year has passed, and I look back and marvel at how the Lord has sustained me. He has not only helped me with all of my deadlines and responsibilities, but I have also experienced a serenity that truly feels heaven-sent.

He has guided me, given me strength, and enabled me to bloom in the midst of the most grueling year of my life. I haven't felt overwhelmed or distraught, and I have even lost fifteen pounds in the process, not from nerves, but by making good choices. Instead of being "buried" by life this year, I am healthier, calmer, and more confident than I was when I started. Only God can do that!

Lord, guide me always for your glory!

Joy Note: How is your garden growing?

A Humble Path

Do nothing out of selfishness or out of vainglory;
rather, humbly regard others as more
important than yourselves.

—PHILIPPIANS 2:3

Contrary to everything the world tells us, humility is our shortcut to happiness. In fact, no amount of worldly fame, material gain, or human acclaim can satisfy our hearts, which are hungry for a lasting truth and an abiding joy. The sooner we understand this, the happier we will be. As St. Thérèse of Lisieux promised, "As long as you're humble, you will be happy."[9]

Other spiritual giants agree with this truth. St. Teresa of Àvila pointed out, "Humility . . . comes with peace, delight, and calm."[10] Pride is said to be the mother of all sin, as Thomas à Kempis warned in his classic *The Imitation of Christ*: "A proud and avaricious man never rests, and the hearts of the proud are filled with envy and anger."[11] And, of course, there is Jesus, who spent his entire public ministry encouraging us to learn from him about how to be both humble and human at the same time!

Still, much of our modern-day stress and strife come from believing that we are not getting the attention we deserve or the acknowledgment that we think we have earned. Every point of restlessness begins with a feeling that we should have more or be more and that others may be better off than we are. All this striving can truly make us miserable.

There's nothing wrong with wanting to do our best and be our best. However, we get off track when our motives are fueled by pride and personal gain instead of humility and love. What do you think would happen in our world (not to mention in our hearts) if for just one week, we all humbly regarded others as more important than ourselves? I think it would make a difference, don't you?

Lord, show me the way to be humble and happy.

Joy Note: What steps toward humility will you take today?

Out with the Old

So whoever is in Christ is a new creation: the old things have passed away; behold, new things have come.

—2 CORINTHIANS 5:17

God is in the restoration business. He can take the most broken-down, dilapidated heart and clean it up so that it looks brand new. He can polish off the rough edges, wipe out the scratches, remove the stains, and put a shine on a soul so that it sparkles brighter than the brightest star. He's done it for me, so he can do it for you and anyone else who is willing to let go of the old to make room for the new in their hearts and their lives.

Our transformation is at God's fingertips—it is his intention for our lives and he is always ready to work to accomplish it in us. However, we have to be willing to let go of all that is outdated and not working in our lives. These could be self-defeating ways of thinking, destructive habits that bind us to mediocre living, or sinful lifestyles that keep us outside the power of his grace. We "lose our luster" as a consequence of living in a fallen world, but God's greatest desire is to restore us so that we can move beyond mere survival into the abundant life to which we are called and promised.

As with any restoration project, it will take time. If we are seeking an instant fix to our lives, it probably won't come. The transformation typically happens layer by layer and will require some elbow grease on our part. First, we "review the plans" with the Project Leader. Then we apply the sacraments. Finally, we take up the task of letting go and letting God change us from the inside out.

This process not only applies to us but also the lives of our loved ones and those for whom we are concerned. From the outside, their lives may look messy, and we may fear that they are beyond the restorative power of God's grace. But they are not. In such situations, let your intercessory prayers be God's primer. God may use your faith to strip down defenses or build up a case for his action in their lives. No matter what, don't abandon the project because God won't, and his finished work will be more beautiful than you could ever imagine.

Lord, restore my life.

Joy Note: What do you need to let go of?

Everything I Ever Learned

Let mutual love continue. Do not neglect hospitality,
for through it some have unknowingly entertained angels.

—HEBREWS 13:1-2

One Sunday afternoon I attended an art show that featured the work of local artists. As I was browsing, I found myself drawn to the work of one particular artist. Each of her pieces was constructed with delicately cut paper arranged to create unique and colorful collages. Each was moderately priced, and it was clear that the artist wanted above all to share her creations with others.

As I was deciding which item to purchase, an elderly woman came up beside me. She shyly but with simple joy began to explain how she had constructed the intricate collages. I was fascinated as she shared the "back story" of each piece and was moved by the obvious love that she had poured into making them.

Still listening, I glanced down at her name tag and recognized the name immediately, as it was an unusual one that I had heard only once in my life. I couldn't hold back the question: "Were you a teacher once?" She barely had a chance to reply in the affirmative when I blurted out, "You were my kindergarten teacher!" With that, tears welled up in her eyes as she confided that she had secretly hoped that she would run into one of her former students that day!

Forty-five years before, I had been her student. I excitedly told her how beautiful I thought she was then and that I even remember the jewelry and makeup she wore because she had always dressed so stylishly. For a few brief moments, we were both carried to a different place and time. Though she was now in her mideighties, I found myself just as enchanted by her grace and beauty.

It is such a blessing when we experience such chance encounters! The verse at the beginning of this reflection reminds us that we may even be entertaining angels along our way! Sometimes life can get fairly monotonous. We go about our routines and responsibilities with our noses to the grindstone, and it's easy to forget that life can also be a great adventure. We never know who God will put in our paths to bring us joy!

Lord, help me to be open to special encounters that are heaven-sent.

Joy Note: How will you stay open to adventure today?

Holy Joy

*I am overflowing with joy all the more because
of all our affliction.*

—2 Corinthians 7:4

Edith Stein, or St. Teresa Benedicta of the Cross, as she's known, was a Jewish scholar and philosopher who converted to Catholicism and entered the cloister to become a Carmelite nun. She ultimately gave her life for love of Christ and neighbor when she was gassed at Auschwitz during the Holocaust. That's a brief biographical sketch of her life, but Edith can best be understood and embraced through her writings. While scholars continue to study her works, you and I can delight in the heart of this beloved saint, which was so devoted to God, through one of her prayers:

O my God, fill my soul with holy joy, courage, and strength to serve You. Enkindle Your love in me and then walk with me along the next stretch of road before me. I do not see very far ahead, but when I have arrived where the horizon now closes down, a new prospect will open before me, and I shall meet it with peace.[12]

Remembering that Edith willingly walked to her death at Auschwitz, this prayer takes on a prophetic meaning. What strikes me are the first few words: "Fill my soul with holy joy." She wrote them knowing that joy becomes holy when it is born of sorrow. Nevertheless, Edith did not fear the cross. She knew its value, especially when it was carried by someone with a joyful heart. Indeed, final accounts of St. Benedicta confirm that there was a "light-hearted happiness in the way that she spoke," and she could be seen "smiling the smile of unbroken resolve"[13] as she boarded the train to Auschwitz.

Our joy, too, can be made holy when we offer it as a gift to the Lord, regardless of our circumstances. We can choose joy instead of despair and wrap it up with whatever threads of trust we can muster. Then we "lift up our hearts," as we are invited to do at Mass, and God does the rest.

Lord, lift up my heart to receive your holy joy.

Joy Note: How will you offer your gift of joy to the Lord in the midst of your trials?

Formula for Joy

Your every word is enduring;
all your righteous judgments are forever.

—PSALM 119:160

Albert Einstein's theory of relativity generated the famous formula $e=mc^2$. We have an equally valuable formula for joy: $j=og^2$! Can you guess what it stands for? Joy equals obedience times gratitude squared.

The theory behind the formula is that joy is the direct result of right living. Obedience to God's will leads only to one thing: true joy. Obedience is made possible, even easier, when it is coupled with gratitude. Gratitude, by its very nature, multiplies itself when it is expressed. And gratitude grows exponentially through obedience!

You can apply this formula to your life. Pride and stubbornness often get in the way of our obedience, but if we remember the formula and walk in God's way, obedience will become a delight. In Scripture there is a virtual ode to obedience in Psalm 119. In most all of its 176 verses, the writer speaks of the joy that comes from following God's laws while praising and thanking him for their goodness. Here are some proven equations for excellent living:

Avert my eyes from what is worthless;
  by your way give me life. (37)

Your testimonies are my heritage forever;
  they are the joy of my heart. (111)

Thus, I follow all your precepts;
  every wrong way I hate. (128)

Lovers of your law have much peace;
  for them there is no stumbling block. (165)

Have you ever heard the saying "Excellence is not an achievement but an attitude"? Our attitude toward obedience can make or break our quest for joy. In church a little boy started running up the center aisle. His father caught him and sternly instructed his son to obey him and return to his seat. The little lad began to wail, and at the top of his lungs proclaimed, "*I don't want to obey!*" Then he proceeded to be miserable for the rest of the Mass. Sometimes we're just like that little boy!

Lord, help me to obey my way to joy.

Joy Note: How will you apply this formula for joy?

Speaking Our Truth

*"Therefore whatever you have said in the darkness
will be heard in the light."*

—LUKE 12:3

Nothing can kill joy faster than an internal dialogue that
is self-defeating or shaming. Yet many of us have these
"old tapes" playing in our heads all the time. Here was
one of mine: "You're not good enough." Here's another,
shared by a friend: "If people knew what you were really
like, they wouldn't like you at all."

I'm not sure where these interior conversations come
from or why they stick around, but they can become
very destructive if we don't bring them up to the surface
and into the light of day— and then send them packing!

We need to press the "off button" to this negative
self-talk and replace it with uplifting, encouraging, and
affirming messages of hope, life, and love. This is something we have to do for ourselves—speaking the truth
in love with our own voices to our own hearts. It might
help to remember that God hears us even when we do
not speak. He sees everything that we try to hide from
others, and yet he loves us, accepts us, delights in us, and
desires us with all of his heart anyway.

Sacred Scripture is a good place to start for affirmations. On page after page, God promises that we are forgiven, chosen for success, treasured, secure, protected, confident, capable, gifted, spiritually alive and free, welcome in his presence, and fearfully and wonderfully made. Here is one of my favorite affirmations :

> For I am convinced that neither death, nor life, nor angels, nor principalities, nor present things, nor future things, nor powers, nor height, nor depth, nor any other creature will be able to separate us from the love of God in Christ Jesus our Lord. (Romans 8:38-39)

Centering our minds on thoughts like these will put the old tapes on hold forever. Scriptural affirmations create expectancy for God's light to flood our souls and lives. They do away with the darkness so that what we say to ourselves will be entirely true and worthy of proclaiming from the rooftops.

Lord, send your Spirit to speak his truth into my heart and mind.

Joy Note: What will you tell yourself today?

Who's Your Daddy?

You received a spirit of adoption, through which
we cry, "Abba, Father!"

—ROMANS 8:15

God could have revealed himself to us in any way: as an energy source, as a mother, or as a king, for example. But he chose to reveal himself to us as a father and made us his heirs and his beloved children. From this revelation, we can conclude that fatherhood is not only important but essential.

When a disciple asked Jesus how we should pray, Jesus instructed him to start the prayer with "Father, hallowed be your name" (Luke 11:2). It's tempting to simply skim over this part of the prayer. But think about it: that we can even address God at all by calling him "Father" is an awesome thing! As the New Testament unfolds, the story of our heavenly Father's love for us is revealed in the life and public ministry of Jesus. Jesus, through his witness and words, shows us that God desires to be close to us as a loving and fully present Father. In fact, he has "adopted" us and wants us to call him "*Abba*," "Daddy"!

When Jesus was saying good-bye to his disciples at the Last Supper, he encouraged them by saying, "Do not let your hearts be troubled. . . . In my Father's house there are many dwelling places" (John 14:1, 2). The truth is that we belong to a Christian family, a communion of saints, and we are always welcome in God's eternal home.

If you have a difficult relationship with your earthly father, God can fill whatever void you might have in your heart. And if you have a wonderful relationship with your father, think of how much deeper your love can be with your heavenly Father. Our adoption into God's family is assured through our baptism. We don't have to be afraid to take God's hand and let him lead us; we can jump into his arms whenever we need a hug. We can rejoice in God's love because he's our Daddy, and he loves us with an everlasting love (Jeremiah 31:3, NRSV).

Abba, Father, I love you with all my heart.

Joy Note: Have you talked with your Daddy today?

Becoming a Joyful Warrior

As pressure and stress bear down on me,
I find joy in your commands.

—Psalm 119:143, NLT

Any time that women come together in the name of Jesus, joy will be overflowing. And that's what happened at an event appropriately titled "The Joy Luncheon." My presentation was called "From Fearful Worrier to Joyful Warrior in 10 Simple Steps," and these steps are actually based on the words from Scripture.

For example, one step suggests that in any given situation, we should train ourselves to ask, "What is the best thing that can happen now?" When we focus on the potential good that can come out of any problem or challenge instead of dwelling on and dreading the worst, we are claiming the scriptural promise of Romans 8:28 that God works all things for good for those who love him.

Another step is a reminder to be prepared to do battle against fear. To be ready, we have to clothe ourselves in the proper attire, as St. Paul says in Colossians. We are to "put on . . . as God's chosen ones . . . heartfelt compassion, kindness, humility, gentleness, and patience" (3:12). These fruits of the Holy Spirit have the power to defeat fear and increase our joy. Further on in this letter, another step is revealed: "Let the word of Christ dwell in you richly, . . . singing psalms, hymns, and spiritual songs with gratitude in your hearts to God" (3:16). This step urges us to never miss an opportunity to praise and thank God. Forming a habit of praise is one of the best ways to combat worry in our lives.

One of my favorite Scripture verses explains the depth and breadth of God's joy:

The Lord, your God, is in your midst,
 a mighty savior,
Who will rejoice over you with gladness,
 and renew you in his love. (Zephaniah 3:17)

Isn't it awesome that the God of the entire universe rejoices over you and me? Knowing this truth, we can conquer our worries with the assurance that no matter what we are going through, God will be with us.

Lord, make me a joyful warrior.

Joy Note: How will you clothe yourself in joy?

Dream On

Whatever you do, work at it with all your heart, as working for the Lord.

—COLOSSIANS 3:23, NIV

People often ask me how I find the time, with my busy schedule, to write books. They also wonder what steps I have taken to make my dream of becoming a writer come true. Sometimes I think they are disappointed when I give them the answer. There are two ingredients that are necessary to make any dream come true: hard work and sacrifice!

Even though I love writing, there are days when the rush of exhilaration that comes from inspiration is replaced with the doldrums of self-doubt and dryness. Even though I'd rather be writing than doing almost anything else, on days like today, when everyone is out enjoying the sunshine, it is a sacrifice.

Ask anybody who has worked toward a dream, and he or she will tell you that a lot of blood, sweat, and tears go into it. Even naturally talented people have to work hard and practice extensively to realize a dream. Through the years of working to make my dream come true, I have discovered that the more difficult the task, the greater the joy in accomplishing it. As William Shakespeare wrote, "Joy's soul lies in the doing."[14] If dreams were easy to achieve, they wouldn't be nearly as much fun!

Once I committed my writing to the Lord and placed it under the mantle of the Blessed Mother, it took on a new dimension and meaning. My dream of writing shifted to a vocation infused with joy and fueled by love. The act of writing didn't get any easier, but it became a way to grow spiritually, and that made the sacrifice of time and energy all the more worthwhile.

If you have a dream, be prepared to work harder than you ever have before and to make a host of sacrifices along the way. But rest assured that when you work as for the Lord, the joy is in the doing, and love will be your greatest reward!

Lord, I offer you my dreams and dedicate my whole heart to making them come true.

Joy Note: What sacrifice must you make to make your dream come true?

Grace Explained

From his fullness we have all received,
grace in place of grace.

—JOHN 1:16

What is grace, and what does it mean for our lives? Most of us have a hard time understanding the concept of grace. Even those who are faithful churchgoing folks might have trouble putting it into words. St. Thérèse of Lisieux provides us with a good explanation:

> Everything is grace, . . . everything is the direct effect of our father's love—difficulties, contradictions, humiliations, all the soul's miseries, her burdens, her needs—everything, because through them, she learns humility, realizes her weakness—Everything is a grace because everything is God's gift. Whatever be the character of life or its unexpected events—to the heart that loves, all is well.[15]

It is hard for us, with our limited understanding, to accept and trust that when life is hard, God is still very much in control. When we are experiencing tyranny, unfairness, or injustice, we find it difficult to believe that

God's loving hand would permit it. But Thérèse's words remind us that everything we experience, every trial and persecution, is a gift from God. If we can shift our perspective and hearts to truly embrace this reality, then our lives become powered by grace and a love that surpasses our own limits and abilities.

When we receive every circumstance as a gift from God, then we move from misery to mystery and from victimhood to victory. In this life we are all in the same boat, heading for the same shore. Even when life rocks the boat in a big way, Jesus is with us, resting and waiting for us to trust him enough to receive his grace and stay calm in the midst of the scariest storms.

One of the best gifts we can give back to God for his wonderful gift of grace is to stay firmly anchored by it, accepting each life lesson with patience and peace. When we do, joy will flow like a mighty river through our lives, and we will be wrapped in the life jacket of his love!

Lord, please help me to remember that for the heart that loves and trusts in God's grace, all is well.

Joy Note: How would you explain God's grace in your life to others?

Joy Net

Their children will see and rejoice—
their hearts will exult in the LORD.

—ZECHARIAH 10:7

Doug is a very funny guy, and that's what makes him so effective in working with the youth of his parish. He calls the Holy Trinity the "Merciful Mafia" and refers to the Blessed Mother as "Lady M" or "Lady Mama" (a play on the name of a popular secular singer). No matter what the topic, Doug is able to capture the attention of his students with his wit and whimsy while teaching them valuable lessons about the truths of the faith.

As a teacher and a mentor, Doug has earned the respect and affection of the young people. Through his humor, he is able to connect with young people, speak their language, and listen with his whole heart to their thoughts, ideas, doubts, and concerns. You might be surprised, then, to learn that Doug is seventy-eight years old!

Doug's success can be summed up best by a quote from Blessed Mother Teresa: "Joy is a net of love by which you can catch souls." Doug is catching young souls by spreading his joy and showing young people that following Jesus can be energizing—and fun. As far as Doug is concerned, humor helps the "frozen chosen" get in touch with the essence of the gospel and the Person of Jesus Christ.

There are two things that we can learn from Doug's example. First, it's never too late to "throw down your net" and start a new chapter in your life. At his age, Doug is just beginning to catch souls and experience a deeper joy through his work with young people. Second, true joy cannot be faked. Kids especially know when joy is authentic and when it is not.

The truth is that while Doug is not always happy, there is always a "fragrance" of joy that he exudes. He can be serious and solemn while delivering a lesson or reverent and rapt while in adoration, but still, his joy casts a wide net. Doug would be the first to say that no matter how clever our words, it will be our joy that speaks to souls and draws them straight to the heart of Jesus.

Lord, help me to cast a joy net upon all those I meet.

Joy Note: What kind of a net have you been casting lately?

Gift Giving for God

Each has a particular gift from God,
one of one kind and one of another.

—1 Corinthians 7:7

If you think you are someone without any particular talent, you are wrong! You *do* have a unique and unrepeatable gift or talent that God is calling you to explore and share with others right now.

If you're not sure what that gift or talent is, think about it. What activity do you engage in that fills your soul and makes time stand still—something that you could do forever, without getting weary? Cooking, building, listening, writing, organizing, negotiating, teaching, running, cleaning, preaching—it could be any one of these or something else.

We might think that God's gifts are better expressed by others, so we hesitate to bring forth our own. Or we may not appreciate the significance of who we are and what we have to offer simply because we've never been encouraged. If this describes you, remember this piece of often-repeated advice: your talent is God's gift to you; what you do with it is your gift back to him. Since every good and perfect gift comes from God

(James 1:17), you can be certain that your gift or talent is good enough.

A woman who was a wonderful artist could never get past the mistaken idea that she was not as good an artist as her mother. No amount of encouragement could convince her of the unique richness and appeal of her work, so her gift went "un-given." Consequently, she remained frustrated and challenged to find meaning in her life. If we don't share our talents, we run the risk of having them dry up, leaving us with an empty "desertlike" feeling until we do. Have you neglected a gift because you have compared it to someone else's?

God doesn't require us to jump through hoops when it comes to sharing or expressing our gifts and talents. He enkindles a passion within us to develop and share our gifts with love right where we are. So what are you waiting for? Give him (and the rest of us) the gift of your unique and particular talents.

Lord, thank you for my gifts and talents. From this day forward, I receive them with joy.

Joy Note: How will you share your talent with others today?

Light and Dark

"I came into the world as light, so that everyone who believes in me might not remain in darkness."

—JOHN 12:46

Jesus tells us that he is light, so when we receive him and carry him in our hearts, we, too, can become a light in the world. This is an exciting proposition because the world is in desperate need of God's light, and we can help to bring it to those who are immersed in darkness. People who come to know Jesus cannot imagine their lives without him; indeed, it would be like fumbling around in a dark room. Without the light of Jesus, life can be confusing, scary, and void of hope.

Even for those of us who follow Christ, there are times when we get overwhelmed with the darkness of this world. If we spend too much time lamenting all that is wrong and focusing on the darkness, we might find that our light is diminished. That's why we need to keep our eyes turned toward the Son. We need to continually let his light into our lives by opening our hearts, like we would open a window or the blinds to let light into a room. Staying with that analogy, if our windows happen to be dirty or stained with sin or discouragement, we can reach out to Jesus and plug into his light through the Sacrament of Reconciliation. Jesus' light is always on, and the power of his love overcomes darkness and is a current that electrifies the world!

Try this experiment as a tangible reminder that light always trumps darkness. Find two stones: one white and one black. Take the black stone and rub it on the white one as if it were an eraser. Does the blackness stay on the white stone? Is the blackness able to "rub out" the white? Next, take the white stone and rub it on the black one. What happens? The white actually scratches out the black and leaves its mark on the dark stone. I have two such stones on my office desk as a simple reminder that light always has the power to "rub out" darkness and that no amount of darkness can ever extinguish the light of Jesus.

Lord, let your light shine brightly within me.

Joy Note: How will you be light today?

Lessons and Love Stories

*"I will open my mouth in parables,
I will announce what has lain hidden
from the foundation [of the world]."*

—Matthew 13:35

Everyone loves a good story. Stories capture the imagination and fill us with joy and delight. Telling stories can help us to connect with one another, and they even have the power to dissolve the differences that divide us. No one knew this better than the Master Storyteller.

Jesus used stories to teach and reach the people of his day. His stories remain the best ever told because they address matters of the human heart with divine wisdom and truth. Some of my very favorite stories are Jesus' so-called nature parables. They employ word pictures from nature and use concepts that are familiar, such as seeds and birds and lilies of the field. Whenever I read this passage, I feel as though Jesus were speaking directly to me:

"Why are you anxious about clothes? Learn from the way the wild flowers grow. They do not work or spin. But I tell you that not even Solomon in all his splendor was clothed like one of them. If God so clothes the grass of the field, which grows today and is thrown into the oven tomorrow, will he not much more provide for you, O you of little faith?" (Matthew 6:28-30)

Pope Francis has been known to speak the language of the people with practical stories that communicate simply and directly to the issues of our day. In this parable, he compares the task of parenting with flying a kite:

Flying a kite resembles the approach we need regarding a person's growth: at some point you have to let the string go slack. In other words, you have to give things time. We have to know the right time to draw the line. But on the other hand, we also have to know when to step back and act like the father in the parable, who let his son go and waste his fortune to have his own experience.[16]

I am grateful for the stories that teach us and touch us with God's love. Aren't you?

Lord, thank you for the blessing of stories.

Joy Note: What is your favorite parable?

Simple Joy

For our boast is this, . . . that we have
conducted ourselves in the world . . .
with the simplicity and sincerity of God.

—2 CORINTHIANS 1:12

Joy can be found in the simplest things: watching a robin build her nest, receiving a dandelion bouquet from a child, taking a walk on a summer's eve, or feasting on a home-cooked meal. Life's little moments are like sprinkles of water that nourish our hearts with joy. In fact, our souls long for the simple, and I think that is why God gave us the sacraments.

The sacraments are the straight and simple path toward God; through them we encounter his awesome mystery. For example, in the Eucharist we receive Christ's presence and the power of his whole self. In what appears to be simple bread and wine, God makes himself small so that he can be one with us.

We know that our lives can become intolerably complex, that we can run into complications just getting out of bed in the morning! My friend Sara finds a way to keep it simple by going to Mass and adoration several times a week. "I couldn't survive without it!" she says.

She finds the ritual and routine of the Holy Mass to be comforting, yet she is also moved as she contemplates the deep mystery of the Eucharist and the presence of God so near.

If we are looking for joy, we will rarely find it in the outwardly dramatic or spectacular. Joy can often be found in those simple, nearly hidden places, sometimes off our beaten path. A Quaker song for children expresses this idea:

'Tis a gift to be simple, 'tis a gift to be free,
'Tis a gift to come down where we ought to be.
And when we find ourselves in a place just right,
'Twill be in the valley of love and delight.[17]

We don't often think of the valley as a place of delight, but perhaps it is when we are stripped of all of our nonessentials and embrace a spiritual austerity that keeps our souls singing with simplicity and joy.

Dear Lord, show me how to keep it simple!

Joy Note: What simple joy can you celebrate today?

How Does a Tree Sing?

Break forth . . . into song, / forest, with all your trees.

—ISAIAH 44:23

Scientists have found that trees actually make noises when they are thirsty. The noises sound like popping corn but are ultrasonic, with frequencies one hundred times faster than the human ear can hear. Very soon a device will be available to help us interpret "tree speak"!

This research may definitively answer the age-old question "When a tree falls in the woods, does it make a sound?" But it seems as if the prophet Isaiah already knew the answer centuries ago when he told the trees of the forest to break into song to praise God!

And if the trees are commanded to praise God, then how much more are we called to do so? Indeed, our souls are created to soar on wings of praise. We lift them up to heaven, to where we hope they will return, to join all of the choirs of angels in songs of thanksgiving and praise to God for all eternity. In this way, every time we offer praise to God, we bring a little piece of heaven to earth.

As we say at Mass, it is right to give God thanks and praise, and the psalms tell us why:

The LORD is my strength and my shield,
    in whom my heart trusts.
I am helped, so my heart rejoices;
    with my song I praise him. (Psalm 28:7)

I will bless the LORD at all times;
    his praise shall be always in my mouth. . . .
I sought the LORD, and he answered me,
    delivered me from all my fears.
Look to him and be radiant,
    and your faces may not blush for shame.
(Psalm 34:2, 5-6)

Clearly, praise is good for us. It helps us to trust, relieves our fears, fills us with joy, and delivers us from shame. No wonder praise is so important and vital to our spiritual health and well-being.

So whether it is "tree speak" or a joyful noise made unto the Lord, let us give glory and praise to the Lord!

Lord, I love to sing your praises!

Joy Note: How do you praise the Lord?

A Heavenly Recharge

*"Come away by yourselves to a
deserted place and rest a while."*

—MARK 6:31

When the going gets tough, I typically take a nap. I find it to be the single most productive action I can take when I find myself stuck or am confronted with a problem that I just can't seem to solve. Jesus gave the same advice to his disciples when they were being inundated with people and overwhelmed by how to meet their needs. Instead of suggesting they ramp up to hyperspeed, Jesus told them to go off and rest.

That same solution might be applied to our own times, especially if the deserted place to which we go is the nearest adoration chapel. There we find rest of a different kind, the kind that seeps into our souls and brings great peace. At the same time, we will be solving the world's problems in the deepest and most mysterious of ways—by praying and adoring God in sacred silence. It's hard to fathom, but the most powerful and effective thing we can do in the face of life's ills is to go in trust and quietly visit Jesus in the tabernacle.

The time spent with our Eucharistic Lord is a dynamic and soulful respite because it connects us with the power of grace. Just as a power nap can bring refreshment and a whole new perspective, so going to adoration can energize our spirits and equip us for the journey. Blessed Mother Teresa instructed her sisters to spend two hours each day, at sunrise and sunset, in adoration. Bishop Fulton J. Sheen observed a holy hour of adoration every day of his priesthood and said, "The Holy Hour becomes like an oxygen tank to revive the breath of the Holy Spirit in the midst . . . of the world."[18]

As Catholics, we are so blessed to know where to find a heavenly recharge when we need it—at the feet of Christ, who is waiting just for us in the tabernacle to come away and rest a while with him.

Thank you, Jesus, for being my rest.

Joy Note: When will you make your next holy hour?

The Teacup Lady

For Christ's sake, I delight in weaknesses.

—2 Corinthians 12:10, NIV

Everyone knows her as the "Teacup Lady" because Auntie Linda has one of the most impressive teacup collections around. Being a world traveler has enabled her to bring home some very ornate and elegant teacups. She has them in all colors, shapes, and sizes, with some that seem too beautiful to touch and others that are most certainly one of a kind.

One day while I was admiring Auntie Linda's teacups, she shared a secret with me. With a twinkle in her eye and a hint of pride, she declared that every one of her teacups had a flaw in it. Each cup had been chosen for her collection, she said, not because it was in mint condition, but because it had some tiny (or not so tiny) imperfection. Indeed, upon closer inspection, I could find tiny chips or cracks or places where one had been glued or another had been repainted.

When I looked at her with puzzlement, she offered an explanation. "This teacup collection reminds me of how fragile and imperfect each one of us is and how, even though we have our flaws, we are all still beautiful to God!" She went on to say, "I wouldn't trade any one of these teacups for one in pristine condition, and that's just how our Lord feels about us."

There were many important lessons to be learned from Auntie Linda's teacups. Even though we may think that our flaws are obvious and glaring, there is a good chance that others will overlook them or not even take notice. God himself is more caught up with our beauty than our imperfections, so all the time and energy that we put into pretending that we are in "mint" condition could be better spent.

We can even be like Auntie Linda and delight in the fact that we are less than perfect because our imperfections are what make us unique and different from one another. Instead of covering up our chips and dents, we can embrace the ways in which our weaknesses lead us to humility and remind us that our worth is immeasurable in the eyes of Jesus.

Lord, thank you for loving me, flaws and all.

Joy Note: How will you delight in your imperfections?

Excellence Is . . .

Be transformed by the renewal of your mind.

—ROMANS 12:2

Jane is a girls' high school basketball coach. To motivate her players, she uses one of her favorite slogans: "Excellence is an attitude." She has found that statement to be true time and again as she encounters students of mediocre talent but with positive attitudes who surpass the achievements of those with exceptional natural abilities. She has proof that the way that we look at the world and how we approach problems and obstacles can have a much greater impact on our ultimate success than the level of our education or our natural gifts and talents.

There is an undeniable link between what we think, how we feel, and the actions we take. This chain reaction can unfold in our lives to bring about great success or astounding defeat, depending on the quality of our thoughts. If we start out with thoughts that are distorted, inaccurate, negative, or self-defeating, we can be at a great disadvantage. On the contrary, if our thoughts are affirming, positive, encouraging, or self-motivating, we can achieve excellence in everything we undertake.

How we choose to think about things is always within our control. But sometimes we act as though we have no control over our thoughts at all! Instead, we let our moods get the best of us. Our ever-changing emotions can become like rogue cancer cells, devouring our peace and wiping out our sense of balance. Sometimes we need to step back and think about what is causing our emotions. For example, maybe we feel insecure. Insecurity usually stems from inaccurate thinking that belies the truth that our security is always assured in our unchanging and faithful Lord.

Living in excellence, with an attitude to match, requires a true renewal of our minds in Jesus. We need to hand over our thoughts so that each one can be held captive by him (2 Corinthians 10:5). Taking this first step toward transforming our thoughts will get us closer to where we want to be in life and can ultimately take us farther than we ever thought we could go.

Lord, transform my thoughts to bring excellence and peace to my life.

Joy Note: What are you thinking?

Our Daily Mission

"The kingdom of God is at hand for you."

—LUKE 10:9

Scripture tells us of a time when Jesus sent out seventy-two of his followers to "every town and place he intended to visit" (Luke 10:1). This is pretty amazing in itself, because we wouldn't think that Jesus needed an advance team! Nevertheless, he engaged his followers, gave them their marching orders, and equipped them to bring his good news to the people.

To prepare them, Jesus delivered a list of instructions: take nothing with you; offer peace to each household; stay put in one home and don't travel from place to place; cure the sick, accept provision when offered; and take your leave if people are unwelcoming. He even told them what to say: "The kingdom of God is at hand for you" (Luke 10:9).

I can just imagine the seventy-two, whom he sent out in pairs, as they approached each town with fire in their hearts and a sense of anticipation of what the Lord would do through them. The Bible tells us that upon their return, they were amazed and filled with joy. They were truly on a spiritual high and riding a wave of wonder at what they were able to accomplish in Jesus' name. Jesus listened as they recounted how the demons had submitted to them and how they were able to work miracles. And the Scriptures also say that Jesus "rejoiced [in] the holy Spirit" and marveled at how God had worked through his followers (Luke 10:21).

Jesus still invites us to carry out his mission in our world today by sharing the story of his grace and action in our lives. That can be as simple as telling a friend about a time when we felt Jesus' presence in a profound way or offering to pray with someone who is hurting or in need of healing. Both of these activities may be just outside your comfort zone, but it's worth the stretch. Think about Jesus greeting you with joy in his heart and open arms when you return from your mission. Isn't it worth the discomfort and awkwardness to know that he will be so pleased by your efforts to help his kingdom come?

Jesus, I accept your invitation to go out and minister to others in your name.

Joy Note: How will you share Jesus today?

God Moments

*"It is your Father's good pleasure to give
you the kingdom."*

—LUKE 12:32, KVJ

Joy is going on retreat with a friend! I am writing this
reflection as I take a short respite from work and home
responsibilities with a dear friend at a local retreat house.
It is an old and beautiful ivy-covered brick mansion that
sits on top of a secluded wooded hill on the outskirts of
my hometown. It is a treasure to be blessed with such a
magnificent Catholic retreat house nearby, and this time
we even have the whole place to ourselves!

Last evening we sat in the garden at dusk and watched
two young deer prance around just a few yards in front
of us as the full moon rose in the sky. It was so rich to
drink in the beauty of God that surrounds us in nature
and to share in a heart-to-heart conversation with a good
friend. I thought to myself, "If heaven is anything like
this, I can't wait to get there!"

Times like these remind me that God will often give
us tiny glimpses of heaven on earth. If we open ourselves,
take the time needed, and live with expectant hearts,
we can experience these "God moments," which are

wrapped with ribbons of joy. Sometimes they happen in prayer, but mostly they unfold in the course of our daily lives, often when we least expect it. I think of them as moments when God reaches out to get our attention by gently knocking on the door of our hearts. It's as if he's saying, "See how much I love you?"

I love that the Scriptures recount so many times when Jesus enjoyed the company of friends. Just as we do, he experienced all the good things about being human as he drew strength and love both from his Father and through the relationships he had with others. God gives us our earthly home and the gift of those we love as preparation for the riches and bounty of the banquet that we are meant to share with him in heaven. It is important for us to be enriched and stirred by the beauty of each "God moment" that we are given here on earth.

Blessed God, I delight in your love, moment by moment.

Joy Note: Is your heart expecting a "God moment"?

Got Authenticity?

"This one shall be called 'woman.'"

—GENESIS 2:23

I love being a woman, and I especially love being a Catholic woman because it is through my faith that I have come to truly appreciate the deep mystery and joy of my feminine nature. I have come to understand that I am called to be a life bearer who possesses a warrior spirit and a servant's heart. With Mary as my model, I pray to be clothed in gentleness and propelled by love. I strive to embody a quiet spirit that is nevertheless strong and resolute. Essentially, I seek to be an authentic woman after God's own heart.

For me, the greatest joy about being a woman comes from being a mother, but for many years I didn't know if I'd ever be able to have a child. When the doctor told me that I couldn't get pregnant, it was a difficult reality to embrace. I prayed and prayed for a miracle, all the while believing that it was possible. After seven long years, God did answer my prayer with a daughter who is now eighteen years old.

But during those years when I was yearning for motherhood, God showed me how I was blessed to offer my maternal gifts in a spiritual way to others. Every woman has these gifts because God has written them on her heart, and they are present and available even when physical motherhood is not possible. A life bearer is someone who affirms, encourages, and helps others to live more deeply and joyfully. In a special way, women are equipped to enkindle life and inspire others to reach their fullest potential. Spiritual motherhood is a genuine opportunity for women to share their gifts with others in a powerful and much-needed way in our world today.

Authentic women are born and not made. They are living out their deepest truth: that they are created in the image and likeness of God and that they are fearfully and wonderfully made. That is the reality that brings us joy. It's time to recover that truth for our sake and for the sake of generations to come.

Lord, raise up authentic women who know their call to bring life to others through a civilization of love in the world.

Joy Note: How can you share your authentic feminine gifts with others?

How Do You Love?

The greatest of these is love.

—1 CORINTHIANS 13:13

In his homily at Mass one Sunday, the priest asked a very simple and direct question: "How do you love?" It seems as if we should have a ready answer to that question. Yet many of us have to stop and think about how or in what manner we offer love to others.

Even though love is the central call of our lives and the vocation of every Christian, many of us remain confused about it. Sometimes we mix up love with flattery, indulgence, or control. Other times our best efforts to love still end up hurting others or pushing them away. When we stop to examine how we love, it often becomes clear that our efforts can sometimes fall miserably short.

Yes, how we humans love can be quite imperfect. But God's love is not. His perfect love is what guides us, so in order to love more like God, we need to study his love, pray for it, and make room for it in our hearts. Scripture reminds us that "we love because he first loved us" (1 John 4:19). Though never worthy of it, we are called to be bearers of God's perfect love in this world. Since we know God's love best through a Person, we are called to be like Jesus, not by doing everything perfectly, but by striving to do everything with *his love* in our hearts.

As a result of that homily, I prayed in earnest to the Holy Spirit to show me specifically how I should love. I received three answers through prayerful journaling that I don't believe were meant for me alone. First, to love others I need to bring them the truth by bringing them the Truth, who is Jesus. Second, I need to allow myself to be used for God's purposes *first*, before I do anything else. Third, I need to see others as Jesus is calling them to be, not how they are currently behaving.

Because I don't think I'm clever enough to come up with those ways on my own, I am confident that they came from the Holy Spirit! Every one of them would be a challenge if I were trying to love by my own power. Thankfully, I don't have to—and neither do you!

Holy Spirit, help me to love as you do.

Joy Note: How do you love?

Celebrate the Now

"Do not worry about tomorrow."
—MATTHEW 6:34

Pamela was struggling with the steady and swift decline of her father to dementia. It seemed that each week he was fading that much further away from her. In grieving each new loss, she could not help but anticipate the next one, and the burden of her sadness began to overwhelm her. As she was sharing her feelings with a friend, one piece of advice seemed to penetrate her heart: slow it down.

As her friend shared her wisdom, Pamela immediately thought of a film she had seen in slow motion. It reminded her of how many details she had missed when the movie was running on normal speed. Sometimes life's "normal" speed can be too fast. When we slow it down, we become more deliberate about how we spend our time and how we focus our thoughts.

For Pamela and for many of us, the hard times and upward climbs of our lives demand a slower pace. We cannot expect the same level of productivity or accomplishment when we are trying to work through difficult situations or emotions. And if we fail to slow down, we will miss the hidden treasures that are there for us to discover, even in the midst of our trials.

Pamela did slow it down. For her that meant surrendering her worry and making the most of each moment she had left with her father. Every time a "what if" crept into her mind, she pushed it down and told herself to celebrate the now. She let go of nostalgia and put blinders on what was to come. By doing so, she learned to cherish every bit of the journey that she and her father were taking together.

"The now is a simple gift that either we are there to receive or we are not," spiritual author and psychologist Robert J. Wicks has written. "In our lives we have only so much time to appreciate what is before us."[19]

Dear Lord, help me to live moment to moment with you.

Joy Note: How will you celebrate the now?

The Theology of Risk

"How narrow the gate and constricted the road that leads to life. And those who find it are few."

—Matthew 7:14

Mother Angelica, the founder of the Eternal Word Television Network, is a visionary known for her practical, down-to-earth spirituality. She humbly and boldly guided the development of her global media apostolate from the ground up. Her homespun wisdom, coupled with a quick wit, flowed from a childlike faith that was rooted in a deep love for Jesus.

One of the most significant things that she has said throughout her ministry is how she started EWTN with virtually nothing but a prayer and a vision. She has spoken often of the theology of risk. This is her advice:

> Never put a lid on God. You can't give God a thimble and expect a quart. . . . Your plans, your projects, your dreams have to always be bigger than you, so God has room to operate. . . . Get good ideas, crazy ideas, extravagant ideas. Nothing is too much for the Lord to do— accent on "the Lord."[20]

Mother Angelica is a prime example of the way in which God can work through ordinary people to accomplish extraordinary things. So many times we are tempted to keep our dreams small and contained. Yet we have to be willing to do the hard things in life, those things that are well beyond our natural abilities and may even be declared impossible because, as Mother Angelica explains, "God expects his people to do the ridiculous so He can do the miraculous." [21]

Dreaming big is virtuous, and working hard is imperative. When we put these two together, it is assured that God will get the glory because we know that what we accomplish is *his* doing. The loftier the goal, the more room there is for the Lord to work and for the Holy Spirit to flow. There's no greater joy than being a part of something that simply blows the lid off of anything that we could have done on our own!

Lord, give me the courage to do the extraordinary for your glory.

Joy Note: How will you put into practice a "theology of risk"?

God's "Re" Words

The word of God is living and effective.

—HEBREWS 4:12

I love God's "re" words: "refresh," "revive," "renew," "redeem." I'm sure there are more, but these stand out as reminders of God's powerful promises of revision and reconciliation (two more "re" words) in our lives.

For example, in his letter to Philemon, St. Paul writes from prison, "Refresh my heart in Christ" (1:20), calling to mind a refreshing breeze or the Holy Spirit fanning a weary soul. When we are faltering in faith, we can ask Jesus to nourish us with his Spirit. Even in the direst of circumstances, St. Paul found refreshment in the Lord, and we can too.

This promise can also reassure us: "They that hope in the LORD will renew their strength, / they will soar on eagles' wings; / They will run and not grow weary, / walk and not grow faint" (Isaiah 40:31). Life can definitely feel like a race sometimes, and weariness seems to be a hallmark of modern living, but for those who claim this promise and place their hope in Jesus, renewal is an ever-present option.

Sometimes we need to go a step further and seek revival. To "revive" means to bring back to life. When life knocks us down so far that we don't know how to get up, or when the burdens of sorrow, loss, or guilt have caused us to feel as if a part of us has died, we need to claim God's promise of revival as spoken through the prophet Isaiah: "I dwell in a high and holy place, / but also with the contrite and lowly of spirit, / To revive the spirit of the lowly, / to revive the heart of the crushed" (57:15).

Isn't it awesome that God is so near to us in our sorrow and that his intention is to give us new life from the inside out?

God spoke to Moses, promising to redeem the Israelites by his outstretched arm (Exodus 6:6). Likewise, our redemption comes through the outstretched arms of Jesus on the cross. Through him, God's words of promise remain alive today.

Heavenly Father, your promises of refreshment, revival, renewal, and redemption bring great joy!

Joy Note: What "re" word will you put in motion today?

Walking in Truth

"You will know the truth, and the truth will set you free."
—John 8:32

It seems as if we live in the land of a thousand truths. Our culture appears to be driven to erase the reality of absolute truth as it relentlessly blurs the lines between right and wrong. As a result, all kinds of confusion and chaos have filtered into our society, leading to much heartache and pain. In the Church resides the fullness of truth, and that is why we Catholics have a special call in our lives to know and share the truth.

Now more than ever, there is an urgent need for truth to be explained and proclaimed. To that end, Pope Benedict XVI declared a Year of Faith as an invitation for all of us to become immersed and versed in the truth so that we could share it with others. That year, which began in October 2012 and ended in November 2013, was meant only as spiritual jumping-off point for a lifelong quest to know, embrace, and live for truth.

Jesus tells us that knowing the truth sets us free (John 8:32). It's freedom that enables us to stand firm in conflict, know ourselves in the light of Christ, and love in a life-giving way. The psalmist wrote this:

Teach me your way, O LORD,
    that I may walk in your truth;
    give me an undivided heart to revere your name.
(Psalm 86:11, NRSV)

Keeping our hearts and minds undivided and focused on the truths of our faith requires that we seek out opportunities within our parishes or dioceses to learn more about Catholic teachings and doctrine. Two other places we can go are the Vatican website (www.vatican.va) and the *Catechism of the Catholic Church*. Ask your priest or director of religious education for resources for adult faith formation, or take a peek at what your children are learning through their religious education program. It doesn't matter where you start, just that you do begin to make learning the truth a priority.

The freedom that comes from knowing the truth is undeniable, and so is the joy that flows from walking in it!

Dear Lord, teach me your truth.

Joy Note: What truth of the faith will you learn more about today?

A Perfect Combination

Rejoice always. Pray without ceasing.

—I THESSALONIANS 5:16-17

There are two things that make the devil flee: prayer and praise. Together, it is a spiritual one-two punch that results in a knockout for evil every time. And while there are many ways to pray, the Bible especially highlights four qualities that should characterize our prayer: specificity, intentionality, expectancy, and passion.

A specific prayer gets to the heart of the matter. Jesus prayed many specific prayers for others during his public ministry and on his own behalf in the Garden of Gethsemane (Luke 22:42). Jesus also reminds us that whatever we ask in his name, he will do (John 14:13). A specific prayer is always a powerful one because it also highlights our intentions.

An intentional prayer is prayed with purpose and underscores the sense of this Scripture passage: "And we have this confidence in him, that if we ask anything according to his will, he hears us" (1 John 5:14). We pray knowing that we are loved and listened to by a good and gracious God, and we know that his glory will shine through the situation.

Praying expectantly is a habit that we should all embrace. Jesus is quite clear when he says, " I tell you, all that you ask for in prayer, believe that you will receive it and it shall be yours" (Mark 11:24). This is an awesome reality that unleashes the power of faith in a mighty and miraculous way.

Finally, we should pray with passion as we pour out our hearts before God (Psalm 62:9). When we do so, we ignite our praise so that in everything, by prayer and petition, with thanksgiving, we make our requests known to God (Philippians 4:6).

We can rejoice always knowing that God loves us, wants our very best, and desires to answer our every prayer. In fact, praising God through every circumstance in our lives and praying without ceasing when our world is crumbling around us are the *best* defenses against depression, anxiety, and the powers and principalities of darkness. The Lord will move mountains when we offer our specific prayers with intention, expectancy, and passionate praise.

Lord, hear our prayers!

Joy Note: Have you applied the perfect combination of prayer and praise today?

No More Killjoys

*"I speak this in the world so that they may
share my joy completely."*

—JOHN 17:13

A killjoy is a person who deliberately spoils the joy of others. The three most common characteristics of a killjoy are complaining, controlling, and catastrophic thinking. Thankfully, there are three remedies for these conditions: reflection, reconciliation, and renewal.

When we complain, it never stops there. We start with one small spark of dissatisfaction, but like a raging wildfire, our negativity grows and chokes off the flow of grace in our lives. One complaint can lead to a host of devastating comments and attitudes that snuff out our joy and replace beauty with ashes in our souls.

Some of the "loudest" complaining we do never gets articulated but goes on like a perpetual whine inside our heads. We may live with this cantankerous voice all day long. Intentional reflection and review of our inner dialogue in the context of solitude and silence can help us revise the script of our habitual and destructive thoughts.

Controlling behavior demands that others think, do, or say what we want and need so that we can feel good about ourselves. Deep down, our insecurity leads us to control the thoughts, opinions, and reactions of others—sometimes subtly and sometimes outrageously. We can't enjoy the harmony and spiritual freedom that God intends for us when we are stuck on the controlling channel. People will avoid us because intimacy is replaced with enmeshment, and they will be left with a sense of being manipulated through their interactions with us.

Reconciliation, both the sacrament and through Mass, releases us from the need to control. Pondering the life-affirming connections within the Holy Trinity (three distinct, whole, and unique Persons bound by love) can untangle us so that we can be in right relationship with ourselves and others.

Catastrophic thinking is when we always fear the worst. It destroys our spiritual simplicity and our souls' essential spontaneity. To combat it, we need renewal that comes through a realignment of our priorities. Putting Christ at the center of our attention and allowing him to transform us will put everything in perfect perspective.

Lord, show me the way to reflection, reconciliation, and renewal.

Joy Note: Which remedy do you need today?

How Do You Know?

No one can say, "Jesus in Lord,"
except by the holy Spirit.

—I CORINTHIANS 12:3

Jan is a Spirit-filled prayer warrior with a heart full of love for the Lord. Her relationship with Jesus is based on a long history of trust and surrender. Her life hasn't always been easy, but even during the hard times, she has demonstrated an unshakable confidence that the Lord is always listening and ready to act in her life and in the lives of those for whom she prays.

In fact, many people ask Jan to "go to the throne" on their behalf. She is a true intercessor, and her close relationship with Jesus often attracts others and enkindles in them a desire to pursue that same kind of heart-to-heart relationship with him. Jan would be the first one to tell them that there is nothing special about her and that Jesus doesn't have favorites.

Nevertheless, she seems to have a direct line to heaven when it comes to discerning the Lord's will. She is a real lightning rod for the Holy Spirit. When people are struggling to figure out God's will, especially when they are at a crossroads in their lives, they will often go to Jan and ask her, "How do you know what God wants in your life?" To which she will inevitably respond, "You just know it in your knower!"

Your "knower" is that place within you where the Holy Spirit dwells. It is the seat of your soul and the haven for the spark of divine life and inspiration that comes from living a life of obedience in communion with Christ. We have to keep careful guard of our thoughts and actions so that our "knower" can be accurate and welcoming of the Holy Spirit.

The *Catechism of the Catholic Church* says that "to be in touch with Christ, we must first have been touched by the Holy Spirit." We know what we know because it is revealed to us, first by virtue of our baptism and then throughout our lives, as the "Holy Spirit in the Church communicates to us, intimately and personally" (683). This is a beautiful gift from which discernment of God's will flows.

Lord, I long to know your will! Send your Holy Spirit to be my guide.

Joy Note: Do you know it in your "knower"?

Joy Runs Deep

Deep calls to deep
in the roar of your torrents,
and all your waves and breakers
sweep over me.

—Psalm 42:8

As someone who has battled depression most of my life, I can say without hesitation that joy runs deep. Joy runs deeper than any emotion or circumstance, and it can be found in the darkest valleys of our lives. Joy is that babbling brook that you hear in the distance as you make your way through the thick black forest to higher ground. Joy is that ever-present, persistent possibility in the midst of your pain and sorrow.

We all have a cross, and some say that Jesus handpicks ours especially for us. I don't know about that, but I do know that he invites all of us to take up our crosses and follow him. I couldn't imagine bearing my cross without him. I tried it for a while, and the misery was indescribable. But when we sincerely accept his invitation to carry our crosses, whether they are a physical, emotional, or circumstantial ones, we are halfway down the road to joy.

In fact, when we walk with Jesus, all roads lead to joy. With him, joy always has the final say! Most of our greatest suffering comes not from our crosses but from our avoidance of them. Acceptance leads to joy. Acceptance doesn't mean giving up or giving in; it means trusting that Jesus is leading the way to joy even when we can't see it or imagine it.

If it weren't for my cross, I would never have searched for, sought out, longed for, dug down deep, or taken risks for joy. Instead, I would have skated on the surface of my scattered and fragmented emotions. I would never have expended the energy to go deeper to find the beauty beneath the ashes that is pure joy. Without my cross, I would have settled for coal when God wanted to give me diamonds.

We all have a choice in the matter of joy. The lesson I have learned is not to be satisfied until you have found joy uncovered beneath the rubble of your despair. As surely as God is, joy is there.

Lord, help me to carry my cross to the depths of your joy.

Joy Note: How deep are you willing to go for joy?

The Grace of Tears

I will turn their mourning into joy,
I will show them compassion and
have them rejoice after their sorrows.

—JEREMIAH 31:13

In one of his homilies, Pope Francis, recalling the story of Mary Magdalene at the empty tomb, said, "Sometimes in our lives tears are the lenses we need to see Jesus." He went on to urge the faithful to ask the Lord for the grace of tears so that we will be able to "say with our lives, 'I have seen the Lord,' not because he appeared to me, but because I saw him with my heart."[22] Isn't that a wonderful way to truly see the Lord?

For those who believe in the resurrection of Jesus, sorrow has a purpose. It can be our pathway to joy. When we allow the Lord to transform our pain, we can experience a gladness of heart and victory that we never thought possible. The key word here is "allow." Sometimes we wrestle with God because we don't want to let go of our pain, or we refuse to acknowledge that we are in any pain at all. In the first case, we become too comfortable and familiar with our pain, and in the second, we encase it in denial. Either way, we are not willing to risk vulnerability and look through the lenses of our tears to see the hope and healing light of Jesus.

The grace of tears allows us to see things differently. In the garden on that first Easter morning, Mary Magdalene could not see Jesus clearly or even recognize him at first (John 20:14). But when he called her name, she was given the grace to see her Lord and friend with the eyes of her heart (20:16). For us too, the grace of tears will enable us to see the goodness of the Lord beyond our broken hearts. When we do, our lives are touched in such a way that others take notice.

People need to know that their suffering has a purpose and that their sorrow can be turned to gladness; their mourning, into joy. Our lives can be a witness of faith; our tears, the lenses to a new horizon of hope. Don't be afraid to look past your tears to the vision of joy yet to come.

Lord, use my tears to witness your joy.

Joy Note: What lens are you looking through?

Miracle in the Making

Rejoice in hope, endure in affliction, persevere in prayer.

—ROMANS 12:12

Sometimes when our prayers aren't answered right away, we lose hope because we are more likely to expect a "fast miracle." Yet some of the greatest miracles are the ones that unfold over time as a result of a great effort in prayer.

When God takes his time, we have much to gain. We learn about his love with lessons in trust and hope. When we persevere in prayer on our way toward a miracle, we grow stronger and weaker at the same time: stronger in faith and weaker in our own self-reliance. That is always a good thing.

While you are praying in earnest for your miracle, don't give up on gratitude. Let it be the undercurrent of all your prayers. When I was waiting on God to send me a baby, I praised him for his perfect timing, even though I didn't understand it. I thanked him for the barrenness that I was experiencing, both physically and spiritually. Even though the waiting time left me feeling frustrated and fearful, I kept praying with a grateful heart because Scripture is full of accounts of the power of praise and thanksgiving to work miracles even and especially in the midst of doubt and despair.

The *Catechism of the Catholic Church* has this advice: "Do not be troubled if you do not immediately receive from God what you ask him; for he desires to do something even greater for you, while you cling to him in prayer" (2737).

We rarely know what God is doing through our perseverance, but the story of the Canaanite woman in Scripture reminds us that persistence in prayer pays off (Matthew 15:21-28). She was someone who would not be denied! She cried out to Jesus, followed him, and persisted in engaging him to heal her daughter, even as she was being scolded and pushed away by his disciples.

Initially it seems as if Jesus is being harsh and unresponsive. But then he grants her prayer and praises her for her great faith. With Jesus, we can be confident that there is always a miracle in the making.

Lord, give me the grace to grow in confidence and perseverance.

Joy Note: Have you praised God today?

Stay Awake!

"Stay awake, for you know neither the day nor the hour."
—MATTHEW 25:13

Scripture contains plenty of wisdom on how to live as a disciple of Christ, but the verse above is probably one of the most important ones for our times. That's because there is so much that surrounds us that can distract us or lull us to sleep. Constant busyness, materialism, relativism, and spiritual mediocrity are just a few of the hallmarks of our culture that can lead us to be preoccupied, tired, and unprepared.

Jesus calls us to stay awake so that we will be ready for his second coming. Staying awake means that we adopt a heavenly perspective that keeps our minds and hearts focused on our ultimate goal: heaven. Scripture tells us that God is readying a place for us at his banquet table. We are the special guests at the marriage feast, the ones for whom a room is being prepared in a mansion of grandeur beyond our imagining (Revelation 19:7; John 14:2). In fact, our whole lives can be viewed as one long marriage proposal from God as we get ready to be united with him. Here are some questions to ask yourself so that you can see how your preparations are going:

❦ When was the last time that you had a real heart-to-heart talk with God when he did most of the talking?

❦ What motivates you more and directs your actions: getting ahead or getting to heaven?

❦ What was the last stance you took against popular opinion that was based on your beliefs *as a Christian*?

❦ How often do you consider or care about someone else's feelings and situation before your own?

❦ Do you have a zeal for saving souls?

Your answers to these questions may reveal how ready you are for that day or hour when everything in this world will pass away.

Lord, give me the grace of a vigilant heart.

Joy Note: What must you do to stay awake?

Jesus, Others, and You

*"Whoever wishes to be great among you must
be your servant."*

—MATTHEW 20:26, NRSV

Have you ever heard what "joy" stands for? Jesus,
Others, and You. This acronym for joy highlights the
surest way to experience it. When we have our priorities straight, Jesus comes first, then others, and finally
ourselves.

The Lord doesn't want us to put him first because he
is on some kind of ego trip. He gave us the first commandment to have no other gods before him because he
knows that it will make us happy when we do just that.
When we give the Lord the primary place in our hearts,
minds, and lives—when he is at the center of all of our
thoughts, actions, and decisions—we will be fulfilled in
the deepest sense of the word.

We all have a powerful enemy that is looking to steal
our joy like a thief in the night by usurping God's right-
ful place as number one. The devil is constantly throw-
ing idols in our faces to distract us and scramble our
priorities. He seductively attempts to get us to put ourselves and our own desires before the will of God, just

as he did with Adam and Eve. Keeping Jesus first is our first step to joy.

When Jesus washed the feet of his disciples at the Last Supper, it was the ultimate teaching moment (John 13:1-20). But his actions just reinforced what he had been teaching them all along: that "the Son of Man did not come to be served but to serve" (Matthew 20:28). Throughout his life, he showed his disciples how to imitate him by humbly loving others as he had loved them. Any degree that we can put others' needs before our own will bring us that much closer to a life of joy.

Putting ourselves last goes against our human nature, but there is a beautiful prayer called the "Litany of Humility" composed by Cardinal Rafael Merry del Val that provides powerful assistance. If you recite this prayer with purity and sincerity, you will begin to experience the paradoxical power of self-forgetfulness. Just as Jesus promised, when we lose our lives for his sake and for others, we gain a new life of joy in Jesus (Mark 8:35).

Dear Lord, reorder my life for JOY.

Joy Note: How will you put Jesus and others first today?

Seasons of the Soul

Even those who live many years should rejoice in them all.
—Ecclesiastes 11:8, NRSV

Jim is a cradle Catholic who has loved his faith for all of his eighty-four years. He recently took the time to look back on his life and reflect on what he refers to as the "seasons of our soul." A season represents the "work" of our souls during each corresponding stage of life. Just as the seasons change, so do our spiritual intentions and occupations.

The first occurs during childhood and is the season of receptivity. As children, we are most naturally open, and our task it to learn how much God loves us through the care, nurturing, and teaching of our parents and others. We receive the life of the Spirit through Baptism, stir it into flame through Confirmation, and are sustained throughout by the presence of Jesus in the Eucharist. We don't stop receiving in adulthood, of course, but our main focus as children is to soak in God's goodness with wonder and abandon.

In late adolescence and early adulthood, we enter the season of selflessness. We must learn how to let go of self-centeredness in order to grow in maturity and holiness so that we can bear good fruit. This stage is filled with challenges and is one that we revisit again and again as we grow in virtue by grace.

Adulthood is the season of vocation, when we are immersed in the activity and responsibility of our life's work. The challenges during this phase are distraction, imbalance, and the risk of losing our faith due to the pressures and influences of the world.

This leads us to the midlife phase, which is the season of perseverance. During this season, our bodies start reminding us that we are from dust and to dust we will return! Our health may start to crumble; our spiritual lives may grow dry and arid. However, if we persevere during this stage, we will be wonderfully prepared for the last season: the season of detachment.

Far from being barren, Jim describes this as the richest season yet. Letting go has allowed him to embrace a contentment that proves that the best is yet to come.

Lord, help me to grow through the seasons of my soul.

Joy Note: What season are you in?

Rising Above

*"Love your enemies . . . , that you may be children
of your heavenly Father."*

—Matthew 5:44, 45

The Scriptures are filled with accounts of Jesus dealing
with the same types of stress and bad behavior from others that we encounter in our own lives. Many of the Pharisees, in particular, were filled with jealousy and negativity
toward Jesus and eager to trap him and tear him down.

Speaking to Jesus, they said, "Teacher, we know that
you are a truthful man and that you teach the way of
God. . . . You are not concerned with anyone's opinion,
for you do not regard a person's status. Tell us, then,
what is your opinion: Is it lawful to pay the census tax
to Caesar or not?" (Matthew 22:16-17). Jesus saw right
through their fake flattery and disingenuous questioning
to the intent of their hearts (22:18).

This encounter offers us an example of how to deal
with those difficult and petty people who want to see us
fail. First of all, even the Pharisees knew that Jesus was
a man of integrity and that he played no favorites. In
other words, he couldn't be influenced by the actions of
others, good or bad. Jesus was definitely not a "people

pleaser." Sometimes, in order to avoid confrontation, we try to please others instead of speaking the truth in love. Our first step is to always be honest in the face of evil intentions.

Second, even though the Pharisees had malicious intentions, Jesus remained patient yet direct, pointing out their obviously bad motives while still taking time to teach them. He engaged them in dialogue to lead them away from evil. Jesus was always seeking to help others, even his enemies, by expecting better from them. Through Jesus we are called to demonstrate that same kind of stillness of heart and charity in the face of those who seek to bring us down.

Loving our enemies requires us to be secure enough in Jesus to go against our desires for revenge and pray for the best for those who want to hurt us. It's a tall order, but as children of God, our mission is to become more like Jesus, maturing in virtue and rising above the bad behavior that surrounds us.

Lord, give me the grace to love my enemies.

Joy Note: How are you being called to rise above someone's bad behavior?

Wisdom Works

Who among you is wise and understanding?

—JAMES 3:13

"Wise men speak because they have something to say; fools, because they have to say something." This observation from the Greek philosopher Plato reminds us how valuable it is to seek wisdom in our everyday interactions and communications with others. The Bible takes us even further by pointing out that there are two kinds of wisdom: heavenly and earthly. As followers of Christ, we are called to pursue the heavenly variety. In the book of James, both types of wisdom are described.

We demonstrate that we possess heavenly wisdom when we "show his works by a good life in the humility that comes from wisdom" (James 3:13). The wisdom from above is "peaceable, gentle, compliant, full of mercy and good fruits, without inconstancy or insincerity" (3:17). But when there is "bitter jealousy and selfish ambition in your hearts, do not boast and be false to the truth. Wisdom of this kind does not come down from above but is earthly, unspiritual, demonic. . . . [And] there is disorder and every foul practice" (3:14-15, 16).

Those are some powerful words and reasons to seek heavenly wisdom in our lives. If you don't have a deep love and desire for heavenly wisdom, then I would urge you to pray for that grace because it will lead to a wellspring of joy in your heart. We are told that if any one of us is lacking in wisdom, all we have to do is ask God, and he will give it to us generously and ungrudgingly (James 1:5).

The spirit of wisdom is described as intelligent, holy, unique, subtle, mobile, unpolluted, invulnerable, loving the good, steadfast, free of anxiety, all-powerful, and pure, among other things (Wisdom 7:22, 23, NRSV). Wisdom is a breath of the might of God and the reflection of eternal light, a spotless mirror of his goodness (7:25, 26). Remember, wisdom works in our lives when we seek the ways of God above our own and walk in obedience. Ultimately, wisdom "produces friends of God and prophets" (7:27). I want to be one of them. Don't you?

Lord, infuse my soul with your heavenly wisdom and a desire to walk in your ways.

Joy Note: How are you reflecting heavenly wisdom?

Heaven's Heavy Hitter

*"And I will ask the Father, and he will give you another
Advocate to be with you always."*

—JOHN 14:16

There are at least eighty-five names and titles for the
Holy Spirit in the Old and New Testaments of the Bible,
but "Heaven's Heavy Hitter" isn't one of them! None-
theless, when you think of all of the ways in which the
Holy Spirit comes through "in the clutch" time and again
in our lives, it may as well be. In truth, the Holy Spirit is
constantly at work in our world and in the souls of all
who welcome and receive him.

It is such a blessing that Jesus did not leave us alone
here on this earth to stumble and fall and hopelessly lose
our way! We have a friend, an advocate, a counselor, and
a comforter who will teach us everything, intercede for
us with inexpressible groanings, and bring us life and
peace (John 14:26; see Romans 8:26, 6).

It's up to us to invoke the power of the Holy Spirit
in our lives. His potential and presence are waiting for
your invitation! On the day of Pentecost, St. Peter quoted
from the prophet Joel, who said that in the last days,
God would pour out his Spirit upon all flesh (see Acts

2:17). We are certainly closer to the last days than in the time of the disciples when Acts was written, so we can assume that the Holy Spirit is ready and waiting to be poured out.

The evidence of the Holy Spirit in our lives is revealed most convincingly in his fruit and gifts. Joy is one fruit. In fact, there are nine listed by St. Paul, as well as seven gifts that can be cultivated and claimed for the goodness of our own souls and for the benefit of God's kingdom and his Church (Galatians 5:22-23; Isaiah 11:2-3). They are the tools of the trade of the Heavy Hitter. We need to be his apprentice in all things spiritual.

The *Catechism of the Catholic Church* says that Christ "pours out the Spirit among his members to nourish, heal, and organize them in their mutual functions, to give them life, to send them to bear witness . . . for the whole world" (739). That sounds like a big job. I'm glad we've got our heavenly Helper on our side.

Lord, thank you for the gift of your Holy Spirit.

Joy Note: How is the Holy Spirit working through you?

Forgiveness and Joy

"Lord, if my brother sins against me, how often must I forgive him? As many as seven times?" Jesus answered, "I say to you, not seven times but seventy-seven times."

—Matthew 18:21-22

Forgive, forgive, and forgive again. How many times do we have to forgive? As many times as it takes until we are free of the burden of bitterness and the desire for revenge. When we are hurt or betrayed, it is natural to feel angry, even enraged. We may be plagued by emotional pain, regret, or guilt. All of these emotions are a normal part of our human reaction to situations that leave us struggling to forgive.

However, when we get stuck and nurture a grudge, we etch a deep self-inflicted wound onto our souls that grows harder and harder to lance. When we encase ourselves in self-righteous anger and cast our hearts in the mud of mercilessness, we build walls of hatred around us, driving others, including God, farther and farther away. Joy will never be able to penetrate those walls without the wrecking ball of God's forgiveness.

When we cling fiercely to a guilt-laden shame and engage in self-punishing behavior, refusing to take hold of God's hand to lead us to peace, hope, healing, and mercy, then joy will stay far off in the distance, unclaimed. We have to be willing to forgive ourselves seventy-seven times as well.

Forgiveness is free to us, but it was purchased at a high price. If we deny forgiveness for ourselves or others, we are essentially returning unopened a gift that Jesus bought and paid for with his very life. He endured unspeakable agony to give us the gift of forgiveness. How can we refuse it?

It feels good to be forgiven, and believe it or not, it feels even better to offer it. When we claim forgiveness for ourselves and find it in our hearts to forgive others, it will open a floodgate for joy.

Lord, give me the grace to forgive.

Joy Note: Isn't it time to forgive?

Conquering Fear

*For God did not give us a spirit of cowardice
but rather of power and love and self-control.*

—2 TIMOTHY 1:7

I spent a lot of years in fear. It wasn't a godly fear or reverence but a life-sapping dread that enslaved my spirit and filled me with anxiety. Freedom from that fear was a major miracle of mercy. God moved a mountain in my soul, and I lived to tell about it!

I've found out since that many people live in fear. When we are going through tough struggles, we often think that we are the only ones who feel a certain way, but fear is universal. We all feel it to some degree at one time or another in our lives. Sometimes fear gains a stronghold, becomes a habit, or takes complete control over our lives, and that is when we need to turn it over to the Lord.

It's comforting to know that God doesn't give us a spirit of fear, and he doesn't want us to stay in it. His loving kindness and healing power can help us to conquer our fears. We also need to do our part in facing our fears. A wise woman, Eleanor Roosevelt, once said that we should do one thing every day that scares us. Nelson

Mandela said that courage is not the absence of fear but the triumph over it. Jesus told us to fear not because we will never be forgotten by God (Luke 12:6-7).

St. Paul, in his letter to the Romans, gives us our marching orders when it comes to our perspective on fear:

> If God is for us, who can be against us? He who did not spare his own Son but handed him over for us all, how will he not also give us everything else along with him? . . . What will separate us from the love of Christ? Will anguish, or distress, or persecution, or famine, or nakedness, or peril, or the sword? . . . No, in all these things we conquer overwhelmingly through him who loved us. (Romans 8:31-32, 35, 37)

In the battle against fear, the Lord is our Commander-in-Chief. In him, with him, and through him, we can conquer anything!

Lord, deliver me from my fears.

Joy Note: What have you done lately that you were afraid to do?

True Beauty

Your adornment should [be] . . . the hidden character of
the heart, expressed in the imperishable beauty
of a gentle and calm disposition, which is
precious in the sight of God.

—1 PETER 3:3,4

Americans spend about eight billion dollars a year on beauty products, and it's estimated that in her lifetime, an average American woman will spend fifteen thousand dollars on cosmetics alone to enhance her appearance. This doesn't include what she might spend on plastic surgery, diets, jewelry, or other means to improve her looks.

What does this say about us? Whose attention are we trying to capture? Why is it necessary to improve upon or cover up what God has made? Why are we spending so much time and money on what is on the outside instead of what is on the inside? If God finds our inner selves precious, why can't we? These are challenging questions that are probably worthy of an entire book of their own.

Pope Francis recently tweeted this: "The one who loves Christ is full of joy and radiates joy."[23] Now there's a beauty secret worth sharing! Those who love Christ radiate joy, and that is an assurance of beauty that shines through from our very souls, a beauty that money can't buy. When we are full of the joy that comes from our relationship with Jesus, others are drawn to us, not because of what we look like, but because of who we are and who we love. This is a beauty that never fades.

I can still remember a woman I met who embodied this kind of lasting beauty. She lived in the county nursing home. It was a dismal places, but Lenore lit up the room. Her eyes sparkled like blue diamonds; her snow-white hair was tousled but elegant. A stroke had taken her ability to walk and talk and even smile, but still her eyes would beckon me as she sat there clutching her rosary.

We became fast friends. She was one of the most delightful women I have ever known because she was so obviously full of joy, loving Jesus and the Blessed Mother with all of her being. She never spoke one word, but I knew her heart well enough to hope that one day I would be as beautiful as she is.

Lord, help me to radiate beauty that comes from joy.

Joy Note: Are you ready to let your inner beauty show?

Great Expectations

Love . . . bears all things.

—1 Corinthians 13:4,7

I can still remember the first argument between my husband and me after we had gotten married. We had just returned from our honeymoon, and I felt that he was not spending enough time with me. After all, we were *married*, and that meant we would spend all of our free time together, right? Wrong.

My husband was a little older and wiser than I was at that time. He pointed out that we hadn't always found the same things interesting before our marriage, so why would we suddenly be "joined at the hip" after our marriage? I suppose he had a point, but I was still hurt by what I felt was a lack of intimacy and time together.

What I know now is that my idealistic expectations were bound to collide with the reality of what happens when two totally separate human beings come together as one in marriage. We may have become one by God's grace in a spiritual sense, but we needed to leave room for negotiation and work at it in the temporal realm. Experts say that most marriages fail because of unrealistic expectations. If you are expecting to be happy, fulfilled, understood, and conflict free throughout your marriage—or in any relationship, for that matter—you're going to be disappointed and maybe even grow discouraged and disheartened.

The disciples fell into the trap of expecting Jesus to be someone other than who he was. When Jesus asked, "Who do you say that I am?" (Matthew 16:15) only Peter had the right answer. Most of the apostles were still looking for Jesus to lead a political revolution or rise through the ranks of the religious hierarchy to save them from persecution. The lesson is that when we hold on to unrealistic expectations, we never grasp the true beauty and joy of genuine intimacy.

True love bears all things (see 1 Corinthians 13:7). It requires two imperfect human beings to come together and make the most of it. That means hard work and a commitment and willingness to overlook shortcomings in others and ourselves.

Heavenly Father, help me to love myself and others, imperfections and all.

Joy Note: What are you expecting?

Back to the Beginning

The steadfast love of the LORD never ceases,
his mercies never come to an end;
they are new every morning.

—LAMENTATIONS 3:22-23, NRSV

"Just when you think you have it all figured out, a new mystery pops up; and just when you think you've 'arrived,' you turn around and realize you've only just begun." Those were the reflections of a retiring priest as he shared some final words with his parishioners. New beginnings, he explained, are the hallmark of our Christian walk, and that's why we need God's mercies renewed every morning.

Each time we walk out of Mass or the confessional, each time we start a new day, we begin again to follow Jesus on our journey. It is both humbling and freeing to know that we can start anew and begin again when we falter. It's also comforting to know that we are wrapped in God's mercy every morning when we step out of bed.

Have you ever watched toddlers who have just recently begun to walk? Their tremendous energy and enthusiasm and total spontaneity are infectious! Sometimes they just get up only to fall back down again or go around and around in circles just for the sheer pleasure of it. They don't focus on the falls because they find it so exciting to see what happens when they get back on their feet. They take all of their energy and every tiny muscle and apply them to those next steps.

We are called to do the same. Even when we feel like we're back at the beginning, there is a purpose for it. More often than not, we won't know what it is right away. But if we view each setback as just a step back and a chance to muster up a little more courage, strength, or wisdom for the next leap forward, we'll have the right attitude. With Jesus there is never shame or condemnation in starting over.

Whether our steps take us back to the beginning or somewhere smack-dab in the middle of a new set of challenges, we can navigate the uncharted territory because Jesus is always with us, cheering us on with his steadfast love.

Lord, help me to remember your mercies and the promise of every new beginning.

Joy Note: What do you need to begin anew?

Be the Light

"Your light must shine before others."
—MATTHEW 5:16

St. Catherine of Siena is best known for her zeal and mystical experiences, with the most famous being one in which she exchanged hearts with Jesus. Yet her life was filled with lessons that we can benefit from today. As a child, Catherine was so happy that her family gave her the pet name of *Euphrosyne*, meaning "joy," after the Greek goddess of joy. That joyful spirit carried her through public persecutions, false accusations, and a whole host of other challenges as she worked to reform the Church in turbulent and troubled times.

Here is a simple saying that could sum up the way in which St. Catherine conducted herself: *Lamenting the darkness won't turn on the light.* If Catherine were living in our world today, she would no doubt blaze a trail for us to follow. Just as in her day, many people today are beginning to notice that the world is in a bit of trouble—even those who profess no belief in God or religion.

As a consequence, many people are waking from their slumber and are ready to take action. We have to be careful not to waste our time finger-pointing and grumbling and giving in to the heaviness and negativity. Talking about the darkness won't make it go away. Instead, we need to be like Catherine and find the courage, tenacity, interior wisdom, and spiritual maturity to be the light.

Catherine said, "If you are what you should be, you will set the whole world ablaze!"[24] Your world is the people you encounter every day. How will you be light in the darkness of jealousy, confusion, competition, and mistrust? Remember: complaining undermines virtue, and love isn't possible without sacrifice.

Now, more than ever, we are being called to sacrifice something that we covet most of all: our comfort. It is up to us to bring others with us to the light-filled gates of heaven. How will we do that when we are fumbling around and grumbling about the dark?

Step up, step out, and be the light this world can't live without!

Lord, fill me with your holy fire.

Joy Note: How does your light shine?

Decisions, Decisions

Into the bag the lot is cast,
but from the LORD comes every decision.

—PROVERBS 16:33

Have you ever experienced the inability to make a decision? We can be filled with angst and ambivalence as we try to arrive at the best outcome for a situation that isn't yielding any great hints. We don't usually have to make major life decisions, but even the everyday ones can have important implications and generate many conflicting "what if" scenarios to contemplate. Sometimes the closer the deadline looms for making the decision, the muddier the waters become.

This happened to me. As hard as I tried to discern God's will, I couldn't get a clear sense of what to do. So I mulled over my options one last time and made a decision. Within thirty seconds, I realized that I had made the wrong decision because it wasn't bringing me internal peace. In fact, I felt worse than I had in my ambivalence. Even though everyone around me was quite satisfied with the decision, I knew it was wrong.

So I reversed it, and that's when things got interesting because it was not a popular one. In fact, even though it was the most loving decision I could have made, it wasn't received that way. But as the storm of controversy swirled around me in the aftermath of my decision, I was still at peace—more confirmation that it was indeed the right decision.

The moral of my story is twofold. First, sometimes it is better to make a decision even if it is the wrong one because it can get you that much closer to the right one. Second, the most loving decision may not yield the most loving response. In other words, the right decision for you might feel like the wrong one for another person. That might happen when you make the decision to stop enabling an addict or give your teenager a dose of tough love or say no to behavior that will make you well liked but compromise you morally or spiritually.

My decision was not nearly of such gravity, but it showed me this truth: that all ends well when you make the decision to make the most loving decision you can!

Lord, when I am unsure of your will, give me the courage to decide for love.

Joy Note: How will you decide?

No More Quick Fixes

"I came so that they might have life and have it more abundantly."

—JOHN 10:10

We often fall prey to the promise of quick fixes, one-shot solutions, and magic pills to solve our problems and satisfy our hunger for happiness. Our tendencies toward idolatry keep us perpetually searching for people, places, and things to fix what is broken within us. It is the reason why we are tempted by get-rich-quick schemes and why we believe in marketing gimmicks that are too good to be true. The world is more than happy to supply us with a never-ending stream of idols and easy outs, but Jesus gives us a better way. Through him alone do we have the means, promise, and power of supernatural living that will never leave us wanting.

Jesus is the way, the truth, and the life (John 14:6). He came to earth to show us how to live. It's not an easy formula, but it is fairly straightforward. He said, "I am the gate. Whoever enters through me will be saved, and will come in and go out and find pasture" (10:9). Consider taking these steps toward a life more fully lived:

❧ *Receive the gift of the Holy Spirit every day.* Invoke and invite the Holy Spirit into your heart and daily activities.

❧ *Love and forgive others as the Lord has loved and forgiven you.* Develop the habit of becoming a forgiving person, and you will grow in love by leaps and bounds.

❧ *Be patient in your suffering.* Turn your trials into triumph by offering them up. Don't waste the merit that results from sowing seeds of sorrow for the good of others.

❧ *Listen for and follow the voice of Jesus in your life.* He is your Shepherd, and his is the only voice worth following (John 10:14).

Following these steps *will* bring you lasting and life-giving change. Resist the temptation to look to the world for counterfeit solutions and root yourself in the real promise of eternal and abundant life (John 10:10).

Lord, show me the way to live a life of abundance in your love.

Joy Note: Have you fallen for a quick fix lately?

The Gift That Keeps On Giving

"I will see you again, and your hearts will rejoice, and no one will take your joy away from you."

—JOHN 16:22

There's a great difference between "joy" and "fun." In a recent homily, Pope Francis pointed out while it is a good thing to have fun, if we want to have fun all the time, we are likely to become shallow, superficial, and lacking in Christian wisdom. According to Pope Francis, joy is a gift that fills us from within and rests on an assurance that Jesus and the Father are always with us.[25]

Another wise teacher, Servant of God Fulton J. Sheen, said something similar: "Pleasure is of the body; joy is of the mind and heart. Lobster Newberg gives pleasure to certain people, but not even the most avid lobster fans would ever say that it made them joyful. You can quickly become tired of pleasures, but you can never tire of joys."[26]

I like the idea that we can never get tired of joy. It truly is a gift that keeps on giving, one that cannot be taken away from us. I once knew a woman who had been deeply betrayed by a friend, who was able to say that she could "feel God's winks" throughout the situation, in spite of her pain. In other words, she didn't allow her joy to be stolen away by her circumstances, and she kept on asking God to increase her joy in spite of her pain.

In the same homily, Pope Francis warned that we can't bottle up joy and keep it for ourselves. If we do, "our hearts will grow old and wrinkled and our faces will no longer transmit that great joy. . . . Sometimes these melancholy Christians' faces have more in common with pickled peppers than the joy of having a beautiful life!" Joy is really the outpouring of a generous heart. Joy is meant to be shared, and in that way, it is multiplied. It makes it possible for us to rise above the little things in life, like human pettiness, and keeps us looking up with hope in our hearts and a tireless delight in the gifts that joy can bring.

Lord, help me not to be a "pickled pepper." I want to receive your gift of joy.

Joy Note: How will you open a gift of joy today?

Suit Up and Show Up

Be strong in the Lord and in the strength of his power.
Put on the whole armor of God.

—EPHESIANS 6:10-11, NRSV

My friend Jan gives a wonderful and helpful description of what it means to follow Jesus, especially when we are not sure exactly where he wants us to go or what he wants us to do. She says the most important thing to do is "suit up and show up." What happens next is God's business!

When we "suit up," we have to be ready for anything. God could use us at any time for any purpose. Here's what I mean. Two women were among a thousand Catholic women attending a diocesan-wide conference. At different times during the day, they each approached a table disbursing pro-life materials, and as ladies often do, they each began chatting with the presenter at the table.

During the presenter's conversation with the first woman, she learned that the woman had been praying for years about opening up a home for unwed mothers. This woman had repeatedly received the idea in prayer but had never known how to proceed because she knew nothing about construction, real estate, or how to go about securing a place to welcome the women.

Not at all coincidentally, the second woman came up to the table a short time later and spoke of her desire to use her talent and knowledge of home building to help the pro-life effort. What do you think the presenter did? She gave the second woman the first woman's phone number, and within a week, they were in contact. Nine months later (a time frame that seems significant), the two women had created a nonprofit, harnessed a small army of volunteers, raised half of the funds, and secured the perfect building to bring what they knew to be God's dream of Joseph's House into being.

Two women suited up and showed up for the conference that day, having no idea what God would and could do through them to mobilize an entire community. When God has a plan, we just have to be ready. It's exciting and miraculous what happens when we follow God's marching orders!

Father, I promise to suit up and show up every day for heavenly muster.

Joy Note: Do you have your armor on?

Lesson in Joy

God keeps them occupied with the joy of their hearts.
—Ecclesiastes 5:20, NRSV

If you had to teach a lesson on joy, how would you do it? Other than consulting someone under the age of five to guide you in your planning, how would you tap into the spontaneous, free, and wonder-filled parts of your being? How would you pursue an advanced degree in joy—one that allows you to delight in the little things and look for the rainbow in spite of the storm?

All work and no play chase the joy away, so one way to "teach" joy would be to plan a whole day to engage all of our senses in activities that bring us joy. Our five senses—taste, touch, smell, sight, and hearing—are gifts from God and cause for rejoicing. Yet sometimes we take them for granted and forget that they are specifically designed by God for our enjoyment.

Scripture speaks about all of our senses. We are encouraged to "taste and see that the LORD is good," (Psalm 34:9). We are reminded that "the ear that hears, the eye that sees— / the LORD has made them both" (Proverbs 20:12). The importance of touch is highlighted through the woman with the issue of blood who reached out to receive her healing from Jesus (Matthew 9:21). St. Paul instructs us to be a fragrant aroma of Christ for God (2 Corinthians 2:15). As Catholics, we are especially blessed to have the fullness of our senses engaged through Holy Mass. So a day devoted to our senses could start there.

Next, we could take in music that stirs our souls and lifts our spirits to the heavens or delight in birds chirping or a toddler's belly laugh. What about the comforting smells that bring about wonderful memories? The rich scent of pine and an apple pie in the oven remind me of Christmas. Maybe we could experience a soothing touch that nurtures us, like a loving hug or the feel of a warm summer breeze on our cheeks. God is continuously inviting us to savor his goodness and provision in the world around us through our senses. How would you use your senses to experience joy?

Lord, help me to taste, touch, smell, see, and hear with a joy-filled heart.

Joy Note: What is your lesson plan for joy?

Perfect Prescription

May . . . the meditation of my heart
be pleasing to you.

—Psalm 19:14, NLT

I've noticed that my attention span is getting shorter.
I'm not sure if it's due to my age or the age in which we
live, but I am so conditioned to sift through informa-
tion rapidly or to search for answers with the help of a
search engine that I can barely focus on an article that
is more than a few paragraphs long. Even when I am
highly interested in the topic, I find myself jumping to
the end. And have you noticed that conversations are
shorter, that the top news is no more than a fifteen-sec-
ond sound bite, and that what used to be an average-
length email now seems laborious to read compared to
a few characters in a text message?

As a writer and a former avid reader, this is a problem. But as a follower of Jesus, it is really cramping
my style! That's because growing in faith and seeking
the truth by letting it penetrate our souls take time and
patience. They also require our full attention and the
ability to engage our intellect and the emotional parts
of our being. When the Bible says, "Mary kept all these

things, reflecting on them in her heart" (Luke 2:19), she did so over the span of an entire lifetime.

So now I am back to the discipline part of being a disciple of Christ. I called out to the Holy Spirit to "expand my territory" (1 Chronicles 4:10, NLT); that is, the territory of my attention and mind to encompass the depth of his truth and the breadth of his word. In response, he led me to cultivate the art of pondering through an ancient spiritual practice known as *lectio divina*.

Roughly translated, *lectio divina* means divine or sacred reading. It has been described as "a way of reading the Scriptures whereby we gradually let go of our own agenda and open ourselves to what God wants to say to us."[27] The process allows us the opportunity for total immersion in Scriptures through a slow and deliberate reading, reflecting, responding, and resting in the word of God. It's the perfect prescription for our hyperactive and distracted minds. Try it and see for yourself!

Holy Spirit, lead me, focus me, and penetrate my mind with your truth.

Joy Note: What is your attention span?

Plugging In

Rekindle the gift of God that is within you.

—2 Timothy 1:6, NRSV

When was the last time that you were truly inspired? You know that feeling—it touches you deeply, lifts you out of your daily fog, and gives you a new vision. It's that spark of endless possibility that ignites a sense of wonder within you to stir your soul into action. Inspiration always leads to something else. It's what motivates us to act, create, or devote our attention and energies toward something outside of ourselves.

As Christians, we believe that inspiration comes from the Holy Spirit. He is our breath of life and our spiritual "change agent," bringing about whatever is true, honorable, just, pure, lovely, gracious, excellent, or worthy of praise (Philippians 4:8). Thus, inspiration from the Holy Spirit elevates and initiates; it takes us from "here" to "there," lifting us out of our everyday preoccupations and moving us to higher ground. To be inspired is to be open to awe in the midst of the mundane.

How does inspiration come to you? Where does inspiration carry you? How do you think God wants to inspire you? The spiritual life is all about God's creative power and transforming grace. All that we yearn for and desire, all that we are passionate about, is inspired by God to bring about our greater good and draw us closer to his love. When we are inspired, we are also reminded of our incompleteness, because we notice that there is still much beauty and blessing yet to be known and experienced.

God created us to receive the gift of his inspiration through his Holy Spirit. If you are living an uninspired life, you are doing so by choice because, as St. Paul wrote, "All of us, gazing with unveiled face on the glory of the Lord, are being transformed into the same image from glory to glory, as from the Lord who is the Spirit" (2 Corinthians 3:18).

The creative inspiration of the Holy Spirit is a continuous flow, a life-giving current of God's unending love. Plug into it!

Heavenly Father, inspire me with your creative power and transforming grace.

Joy Note: How will you let God's inspiration change you?

Living Letter

*You are our letter, written on our hearts,
known and read by all.*

—2 CORINTHIANS 3:2

Are you living a life that could serve as a letter of recommendation for Jesus Christ? Would someone hire you to fill the position of "Catholic Christian" based on the job description "disciple of Christ"? Would you be considered qualified to be a member on Christ's team?

St. Paul asks and answers these questions in his second letter to the Corinthians. Responding to the many who were questioning him and his followers about their qualifications to be preachers and teachers of the gospel, he wrote, "Not that of ourselves we are qualified to take credit for anything as coming from us; rather, our qualification comes from God" (2 Corinthians 3:5). When the topic of letters of recommendation came up, Paul simply stated, "You are our letter" (3:2).

We can learn two things from St. Paul's words. First, God doesn't call the qualified but qualifies the called. Second, when it comes to sharing or "advertising" our faith, our actions will always speak louder than our words. It's good to think about the fact that we really are walking billboards of what it looks like to be a faithful Christian. The world is hungry for truth and dying for love. We have the fullness of both with a duty to share. Paul reminds us that we gain our confidence to complete this task through Christ alone.

According to Bill Wilson, founder of the twelve-step recovery program Alcoholics Anonymous, members come to the groups not because they are forced or vigorously recruited but because they are attracted to what happens there.[28] Applying this to our call to a new evangelization, we have to be walking and living in possession of something that others want for themselves. People need to be drawn to us by our actions and reactions to the ups and downs of life. They ought to be pointing to us and saying, "I'll have what she's having!"

What do we have that the world wants? We have genuine joy, authentic love, true mercy, God-given dignity, unchanging truth, and real hope for everlasting life. Let's pray that we will be the living letters that remind others of the truth that is written on their hearts.

Lord, use me.

Joy Note: What message is your life sending?

Dying to Live

You have no idea what your life will be like tomorrow. You are a puff of smoke that appears briefly and then disappears.

—JAMES 4:14

There's a song made popular by country artist Tim McGraw that tells the story of a man who hears that he doesn't have long to live. The powerful lyrics catch in my heart every time I hear it: *I hope you get the chance to live like you were dying.* Catholic author and speaker Matthew Kelly invites his audiences to make a resolution to live the next year as if it were their last. Jesus reminds his followers that whoever wishes to save his life must lose it (Mark 8:35). What kind of impact could these sage prescriptions for living have on a life?

I decided to find out. I knew that I couldn't sustain this approach for a year, so I settled on one month. I didn't tell anyone what I was doing, but every morning when I got up, I considered that the next twenty-four hours could be my last and went about my day with that thought in mind.

This is what happened: I ate more ice cream, but I took longer walks. I talked less and said more. I looked for beauty in all things and found it. I asked for more hugs and gave more smiles. I looked into more people's eyes and saw their hearts. I did less but lived more. I listened as if my life depended on it. I worried less but cared more. I laughed more deeply and cried more freely. I gave less advice but shared more wisdom. I got up earlier and went to bed later. I bought more flowers but gave them away. I didn't miss a single chance to contemplate the moon, offer a compliment, or say, "I love you." And in that month's time, I died to the little things that didn't really matter, and in doing all of this, I truly gained a life worth living.

The saddest thing in life is not when we die but when we never truly live. The passage from James at the beginning of this reflection warns against taking the gift of our lives for granted. Life is short. What are you doing with yours?

Lord, help me to cherish every moment.

Joy Note: What if you had only one month to live?

Blessed Balance

Better is one handful with tranquility
than two with toil and a chase after wind!

—ECCLESIASTES 4:6

Balance is a blessing that is good for the soul. But when I think of balance, I think of the old Ed Sullivan Show that featured a man trying to balance a line of spinning dinner plates on a bunch of poles. He ran back and forth, frantically trying to keep each plate spinning in the air so that none of them would go crashing to the ground. Sounds like life, doesn't it?

There are so many things that we have to keep in balance. We have to balance our responsibilities, our emotions, and our checkbooks. We have to balance our time, our attention, and our affections. Nearly everything worth doing requires a measure of prudence, moderation, or temperance, all of which are virtues of balance. Trying to stay balanced can make our heads spin!

The Holy Spirit is our Helper when it comes to achieving balance because it requires that we practice discernment and detachment. We practice discernment when we take time to turn a light on in our souls to examine our motives. If we are driven, is it out of fear or false ambition? If we are anxious, does it stem from guilt or dishonesty? We practice detachment by embracing wisdom. Spiritual detachment does not mean that we become lukewarm, however. In fact, detachment enables us to engage our hearts in what is worthwhile, necessary, and essential, with freedom, passion, and zeal.

Moreover, spiritual balance is made possible through prayer. Prayer is our safety net when we are walking the tightrope between righteousness and sin. Prayer is the lifeline that tethers us in trust to God's goodness and mercy. One person put it this way: "We are spiritually balanced in proportion to the amount of time we spend contentedly sitting at Jesus' feet."[29] Amen to that!

Balance is rooted in remembering who we are and to whom we belong, but it is also following the advice of Teresa of Ávila, who said that while "it is a great grace of God to practice self-examination, too much is as bad as too little."[30] Oh blessed balance, come!

Holy Spirit, bring a blessed balance into my life to calm my soul.

Joy Note: What needs balancing in your life?

Love in Action

Do not be conquered by evil but conquer evil with good.

—ROMANS 12:21

A wise priest has said that Christians need to be like white flowers in the middle of a mud hole. In other words, the messier the world gets, the better we ought to look. If we lower our personal standards or allow our morals to slip or decay, we will become unrecognizable as followers of Christ. The salt of our souls would lose its taste, and we would become immobilized in spirit (see Matthew 5:13). The world needs us to be better than that.

One way to combat sin is to practice the opposite virtue. One heroic act of virtue can cause a ripple effect and cancel out the sting of a senseless act of sin. We can follow Peter's advice and "let [our] love for one another be intense, because love covers a multitude of sins" (1 Peter 4:8). We still have hope for our world because we believe. We believe because we have faith. We have faith by the Holy Spirit who teaches us right from wrong. That's our bottom line: righteous living in the name of love.

There was a young man who was smart for his age and lived a privileged life. He approached Jesus and asked him what he needed to do to have eternal life. He knew the answer but asked the question anyway in hopes that there might be an easy way out. When Jesus informed him that he needed to go beyond the letter of the law of the Ten Commandments and embrace the spirit behind them, the young man went away sad because he wasn't really up for the task (Mark 10:17-22).

Jesus delivers the same message to us today. It doesn't matter what we know, what we think, or even what we feel. The most important thing is what we do to put our love into action and rise above the muddy waters of spiritual mediocrity.

Lord, show me how to put love into action that heals and helps others.

Joy Note: How will you rise above?

Blissful Thinking

For in this tent we groan, longing to be further clothed with our heavenly habitation.

—2 Corinthians 5:2

Spiritual joy or the joy of heaven has often been described in terms of "bliss." We weren't created to just dabble in bliss but to be immersed in it, because bliss is what we will experience nonstop in heaven. It is sublime ecstasy and a complete and perfect happiness that we can't even begin to imagine. It is what Adam and Eve walked in before the fall and what every human heart longs for until its final beat.

Our longing for bliss doesn't mean that we should walk around with our heads in the clouds all day long. However, it does invite us to raise our hearts toward our heavenly home in contemplation of the amazing joy that awaits us. I think this is why there have been so many stories recently of people who have died, gone to heaven, and come back to tell us about it. Their descriptions are magnificent, and many of them are similar enough to what we are told to expect from Scripture and Tradition to keep our quest for bliss alive.

The *Catechism of the Catholic Church* says that in heaven, we will enjoy "perfect communion with God . . . [and] contemplate him without end" (2550). This "beatific vision" also allows us to see certain mysteries and have all the questions of our hearts answered. We will also be able to see each other and rejoice in the company of those whom we loved and were separated from in death. In heaven there's no pain or sadness and no ability to sin as we experience unending delight in the company of Christ, the angels, and the communion of saints. We also enter into a special source of joy when our souls are united with our glorified bodies.[31] In short, heaven will be our ultimate extreme makeover marked by eternal bliss!

Why not engage in some blissful thinking? It's the best way to remind ourselves of who we truly are and where we are going.

Lord, on my way to heaven, send me moments of bliss.

Joy Note: When was the last time you thought about heaven?

Busybodies

What then does it profit them to toil for the wind?

—Ecclesiastes 5:15

"I know you're busy, but . . . " I hear this phrase many times a day, and it bothers me. Are people making an assumption that I am busy because I have a high-stress job, or are they feeling busy themselves and figure that I must be too? Has it just become an accepted fact of life that everybody everywhere is always busy?

It makes me wonder if I am projecting a pseudo busyness that keeps people at a distance, because guess what—I'm really *not* that busy. I have a lot to accomplish in a day, yes, but I have conscientiously tried to remove the word "busy" from my vocabulary. In fact, I can't remember the last time I told someone I was busy or too busy. It would leave a bad taste in my mouth if I did. I simply refuse to allow myself to fall in lockstep with the frantically overworked and perpetually busy.

For example, I try never to be so busy that I can't stop and have a conversation. I make it a point to look up, listen, or attend to a person, even when I am intensely focused or involved in a project, such as writing a book or performing a task at work. While I haven't perfectly achieved this goal, I think I succeed at it more than half the time. The truth is that busyness is a choice.

I know someone who regularly looks at the clock on his wall during every conversation. Maybe it's a habit, or maybe he is simply unaware that he does it; but he is sending a message that he is too busy to give others the time of day. It remains unspoken, but it comes across loud and clear: I'm busy, and you are not my priority.

There's no one on earth who has ever been busier than Jesus. After all, he came to save mankind, and all we have to do is put in a solid day's work. He never had a moment to himself, no place to lay his head, and yet he had the time to dine with sinners, play with children, and address thousands of people every day. Jesus never complained about being too busy, so why should we?

Lord, let the busyness pass away and my true purpose remain.

Joy Note: Do I steal my joy and the joy of others by acting as if I'm too busy?

Love in the Dark

*God remains in us, and his love is brought
to perfection in us.*

—1 JOHN 4:12

A once popular song by a band called Air Supply is entitled "I'm All Out of Love." Isn't it wonderful to know that for us Christians, it need never apply? With Jesus, we will never be out of love. He never falls out of love with us, and his love is unchangeable, unstoppable, and unending.

That doesn't mean that there won't be times when we can't feel that love. His love never fails, but sometimes we fail to receive it—for a myriad of reasons. People who suffer with depression will often speak of a blockage that prevents them from feeling the positive emotions that we associate with love. People who are grieving or who experience chronic pain can sometimes struggle to make sense of their suffering and mistrust that they are loved. Betrayal, personal failure, sin, and a history of abuse can all interfere with knowing and accepting love. Yet none of that changes the fact that we have love and are loved.

As we grow in our spiritual journey, there may be more and more instances when God's love feels far away. This is not because we are loved any less but because we are being drawn into a more mature relationship with Jesus. Instead of relying on feelings and consolations, we are called to cling by faith and trust to a love that we cannot feel but that goes deeper than we've ever known before. Such experiences pave the way for authentic joy.

Blessed Mother Teresa described this joy in the midst of the intense suffering that she endured through an experience of a "dark night of the soul" that lasted for decades. She wrote, "As for myself, I just have the joy of having nothing—not even the reality of the Presence of God. No prayer, no love, no faith—nothing but continual pain of longing for God."[32] Through all of this, Mother Teresa wrote extensively about joy and was said to embody it by those who were blessed to have been in her presence. God's love is greater than any darkness we carry within us.

Lord Jesus, wrap me in your love and I will bask in its warmth, whether I can feel it or not.

Joy Note: How will you choose to love in the dark?

Freedom from Shame

Look to him and be radiant,
and your faces may not blush for shame.

—PSALM 34:6

We have all experienced the sting of shame. There is such a thing as a good and holy shame, the kind that moves us to sorrow for our sins and fills our contrite hearts with a longing to seek the healing of God's forgiveness and mercy. But we can also be debilitated by the weight of an unholy shame that is never of God.

Unholy shame enshrouds us in self-loathing. It keeps us stuck in a shallow grave of misery, suffocating our souls with hopelessness and despair. It deceives us into believing that we can never truly be forgiven. Consequently, we work desperately to hide those parts of ourselves that we believe are unacceptable and beyond redemption. Unholy shame is an exhausting bondage that robs us of our joy.

Holly is a courageous woman who grew up in a broken and abusive home filled with shame. Believing that she had gotten what she deserved, she entered into one abusive relationship after another. Then she met a kind and patient therapist who helped her to unravel the stranglehold of shame on her life. Holly spent the next several years healing from shame. Week after week, through their every encounter, the therapist gently and patiently reflected back Holly's inner goodness. It was an essential goodness that she couldn't see at first because it had never been mirrored back to her by anyone else in her life.

Holly is a modern-day "woman at the well" (John 4:1-32). Her experience reveals what that Samaritan woman also discovered—that we can reclaim our dignity and be freed from shame through genuine loving relationships, both with Jesus himself and with those who show us the face of Christ.

If you or someone you know is struggling with shame, rest assured that the journey toward mercy, forgiveness, and healing is worth it. Start by praying the Divine Mercy Chaplet, and ask the Lord to send a helper whom he can use to release you from the shame that binds you and restore your radiance from within. Don't let shame have the last word in your life.

Lord, take away my shame.

Joy Note: Do you need healing from shame?

Life in the Spirit

Have . . . the knowledge of the mystery of God,
Christ, in whom are hidden all the treasures of wisdom
and knowledge.

—COLOSSIANS 2:2-3

Even the earliest Christians got sidetracked on their journey to joy. These early followers had gotten caught up in a hybrid Christianity that placed heavy emphasis on human performance while negating the power of God's grace. They were "holding to the outward form of godliness but denying its power" (2 Timothy 3:5, NRSV).

St. Paul also predicted that "the time will come when people will not tolerate sound doctrine but, following their own desires and insatiable curiosity, will accumulate teachers and will stop listening to the truth and will be diverted to myths" (2 Timothy 4:3-4). That has happened in the past, and it's also happening now. That is why it is so important that we live in the Spirit and not in the world. We need to know the voice of the Holy Spirit and follow it.

We can live in the Spirit and claim his power. Paul asks the Corinthians and us, "Do you not know that you are the temple of God, and that the Spirit of God dwells in you?" (1 Corinthians 3:16). The Holy Spirit is our helper and friend. He is a guide for us and can steer us clear of the near occasion of sin and all other false steps when we listen to that small voice within us that is our conscience and his presence in our hearts. Our task is to get to know the Holy Spirit so that we can recognize his voice.

We also want to make sure that our hearts are a welcoming place for him to dwell. We can be sure he is dwelling in our hearts when we are able to let go of our resentments and embrace gratitude, when we stop chasing after counterfeit truths and accept his gifts of wisdom and knowledge, and when we stop settling for mere survival and seek out joy. The Holy Spirit never comes to us empty-handed, and we want to make sure that we are focused and ready to receive all the hidden treasures that he has to give.

Holy Spirit, live in me.

Joy Note: How will you open the door of your heart to the Holy Spirit?

So Long, Superwoman!

Without a vision the people lose restraint;
but happy is the one who follows instruction.

—PROVERBS 29:18

Jill suffered from "superwoman syndrome"—she tried to do everything for everyone. That left her feeling exhausted, frustrated, and joyless. But no matter how hard she tried, she couldn't break out of the habit of feeling overly responsible and then overextending herself. And when things didn't go the way she thought they should, she would end up feeling guilty or hurt. It felt like a hopeless cycle.

She took her heaviness to prayer, asking others to pray as well. When she realized that the main reason she kept falling into the self-defeating pattern of doing too much was because she simply didn't have the skills to do things differently, she experienced a breakthrough. She had not developed the virtue of moderation and didn't know how to practice and apply healthy boundaries in her relationships, including her relationship with herself. It became clear to Jill that she had a lot to learn.

First, Jill developed a vision of what life would be like for her if she shed her superwoman role. She asked herself some "what if" questions: "What if I didn't have to be in control all of the time or have a solution for every problem? What if it were more important to let people solve their own problems than to save them from their mistakes? What if there is value in being vulnerable?"

These questions led Jill to make the decision to trade in her superwoman tendency of rescuer/controller for a new one: that of encourager/consultant. At first it felt unnatural not to take the lead and to sit back as others struggled, but she persevered, one situation and one relationship at a time. Jill began to recognize that many people wanted to remain stuck even with her encouragement, while others became frustrated when she wouldn't take over.

The more Jill changed, the freer she felt in her spirit and the less willing she was to trade that experience for the illusion of control. Over time it became natural for her to say "So long" to superwoman.

Lord, free me from doing too much.

Joy Note: Have you let go of your superwoman tendencies?

Pride and Joy

Pride goes before disaster,
and a haughty spirit before a fall.

—PROVERBS 16:18

We have been forewarned: pride goes before a fall. It did back in Adam and Eve's time, and it still does today. "You will be like gods" was the lie of the evil one in the Garden of Eden (Genesis 3:5), and we are still falling for it two thousand years later.

Not only are we not gods, but we are totally dependent on God for everything. Our desire for God originates with him, "for God is the one who, for his good purpose, works in you both to desire and to work" (Philippians 2:13). Even our ability to love comes from God because "we love because he first loved us" (1 John 4:19).

"God resists the proud, but gives grace to the humble" (James 4:6). This alone is reason to seek to rid our hearts of pride. Because pride keeps us working to earn God's grace, it is a futile effort. It reminds me of the child in the front seat of a bicycle built for two. As he mightily struggles to propel forward, he is totally oblivious to his father in the backseat who is the one peddling to keep them going. It is our Father's strength, goodness, and love that keep us moving forward.

Pride and joy don't mix. Pride compels us to enviously compare our situation to others, to secretly look for their faults while blinding us to our own, and to covet what isn't ours. Pride keeps us restless, anxious, and easily discouraged. Look at your life, and if any of these conditions apply, consider that pride could be the underlying cause.

So what can we do about pride? Nail it to the cross, and practice humility. To "practice" is to perform an activity repeatedly to improve or maintain our proficiency. Applying this to the virtue of humility means that we take every opportunity to trump pride with an act of gentle selflessness. The more we do this, the more we will love our own weakness and dependence on God. We will be like St. Paul, who preferred to boast joyfully of his weakness so that the power of Christ could dwell in him (2 Corinthians 12:9).

Lord, I rejoice in my weakness for your glory!

Joy Note: How will you practice humility?

Refresh Me, Lord!

"Were not our hearts burning [within us]?"

—LUKE 24:32

The title of this reflection is the same one as my first book. It is also the name of the radio show that I cohost with my friend Kathy. On the show, we invite Catholics to share their stories of how Jesus has touched them personally or acted in their lives. They are ordinary people sharing stories of God's extraordinary grace.

Many Catholics feel ill equipped to evangelize, but everyone can share a story from the heart. We do it all the time at family gatherings or in the break room at work. We passionately tell people about our vacation plans or spin the tale of the latest saga in the life of our teenager. So why not talk about Jesus?

People are always amazed when they come on the show. They are filled with fear and trepidation at the thought of filling up thirty minutes of airtime, but we often have to cut them off just to wrap up the show. Through the experience, they come to realize that talking about Jesus is not only easy, but it is what our hearts are made for! We are wired for worship, and when we gather in his name to share his goodness, that is exactly what we are doing.

And we are also evangelizing. We are doing what Christ commissioned us to do when he said, "Go into the whole world and proclaim the gospel to every creature" (Mark 16:15). Jesus said, "Where two or three are gathered together in my name, there am I in the midst of them" (Matthew 18:20). I can attest to the fact that when we are talking with our guests, either in the studio or on the phone, the presence of the Lord is alive and active. He is in our midst!

Can I encourage you right now to tell your story? How has Jesus touched you? Was there a time when you felt his undeniable presence or power in your life? Chances are that there is someone who needs to hear your story. Someone is losing faith or has forgotten that he is loved. Someone is walking down a path that you have already tread. Someone needs to know that Jesus is near to them too. Will you tell them?

Lord, give me the courage to tell my story.

Joy Note: To whom will you tell your story?

Thy Kingdom Come

*"Your kingdom come, / your will be done,
/ on earth as in heaven."*

—MATTHEW 6:10

A friend of mine, Susan, drove me to work one morning by a different route. At an unfamiliar corner, I noticed that she was slowing down. Then she pulled up alongside a young woman who was standing there with a sign asking for money. Susan rolled down the window and handed the woman a dollar. They exchanged pleasantries before we took off again through the intersection.

Susan apologized for not introducing me to Linda, explaining that with most people, Linda prefers to remain anonymous. She said that Linda had shown up on the street corner about three months before, and every time that Susan had passed by without acknowledging her, she felt uncomfortable and unable to forget her for the rest of the day. Susan knew one day that it was the Holy Spirit who was prompting her to stop and offer some money, even though that's something she wouldn't normally do.

The next day Linda was there—and the next and the next. So Susan continued to be obedient to the Holy

Spirit and offer whatever token of cash she had in her purse. It wasn't long before Susan noticed that she looked forward to their meetings.

Through these encounters, the Holy Spirit taught Susan many lessons. She learned that it really wasn't about the money but about making the connection with Linda; it was about looking her in the eye and letting her know that she matters. Susan has no idea if or how these morning meetings will effect a change in Linda's life or heart; she only knows that something is happening in her own. She is learning that what God does in and through us is his business and is also more important than anything we can do on our own. God is building his kingdom through Susan and Linda, one day at a time.

We may not think that we are in the kingdom-building business, but we are! We just have to keep our hearts and minds sensitive to the promptings of the Holy Spirit and then be obedient to him. Amazing and unexpected things can happen when we do.

Lord, use me to build your kingdom here on earth.

Joy Note: What is the Holy Spirit asking me to do today?

Divine Dialogue

"For 'In him we live and move and have our being.'"
—ACTS 17:28

Prayer is God's yearning for us from within and our longing for him in the form of a divine dialogue of the heart. It is a lifting up and a settling down as the Holy Spirit breathes through us as an invisible sigh of the soul. Prayer can move us from compulsion to communion when we surrender to grace and lean our heart's ear into the silence.

Prayer has the capacity to affect both our physical and spiritual realities. Spiritually, prayer draws our souls into greater union with God. In the physical world, prayer changes things. Prayer has stopped wars, healed the sick, protected those in danger, reconciled broken relationships, and according to Jesus, it can even move mountains (Matthew 21:21).

While contemplating the power of prayer, the Christian mystic Julian of Norwich received these words from the Lord: "I am the ground of your praying. I put your yearnings in your heart. It's my will you should pray for them, and if you pray, why wouldn't you have what you pray for?"[34] Thomas Merton put it another way:

> In prayer we discover what we already have. You start where you are and you deepen what you already have, and you realize that you are already there. We already have everything; but we don't know it and we don't experience it. Everything has been given to us in Christ. All we need is to experience what we already possess.[34]

Both of these contemplatives, as they grew in understanding and holiness, came to believe that in prayer the relationship with Christ is more important than the results and that the practice of praying is more important than the end product. Their focus was solely on the One to whom they prayed, the One who initiates prayer in the first place.

If you were to consider that prayer is our response to God's desire for dialogue with us, how would you approach prayer differently? What role would joy play in your prayer life?

Lord, let prayer be the secret language of my heart.

Joy Note: What is God saying to you in prayer?

Heaven's Handiwork

For we are his handiwork, created in Christ Jesus.

—Ephesians 2:10

There is something very beautiful and humbling about the fact that we are the handiwork of God. I think of all the love that my mother put into the clothes she made for me when I was a child or the love with which my grandmother carefully crocheted afghans for her five granddaughters. How much more does God pour his love into our being? We are his beloved creatures, his chosen ones. We are made in his image, each a unique expression of his creative love and a reflection of his joy. As the psalmist wrote:

> You formed my inmost being;
>   you knit me in my mother's womb.
> I praise you, because I am wonderfully made.
> (Psalm 139:13-14)

No matter what we look like on the outside, we are beautiful and precious to God. As I am writing this reflection, my mother is in the later stages of a dementia that has taken away her memory and personality.

She finds it hard to speak and seems very far away. She recognizes me as someone she knows but doesn't really understand that I'm her daughter.

To others, it might seem as if she is "no longer there," but I believe that she is. I believe her soul is shining more brightly than it ever has. God knew, even before my mother took her first breath, when her last one would be. He has not stopped forming her or drawing her to himself. The action of his mercy and grace is just more hidden now, like it was when he first formed her in her mother's womb.

We are made for a purpose that doesn't end in our later years. Our abilities may fade away, our faculties may grow dim, but our souls are still the vibrant creation of a good and loving God. We can say with confidence, as St. Paul did, that "although our outer self is wasting away, our inner self is being renewed day by day" (2 Corinthians 4:16).

Lord, continue your handiwork in me.

Joy Note: How will you express the joy of God's handiwork in you and in those you love?

The Joy of Friends

"I do not call you servants any longer, . . .
but I have called you friends."

—JOHN 15:15, NRSV

A book on joy could not be complete without a reflection on friendship. Friends are the family you choose, and when those friendships are spiritual in nature and centered on Christ, they are the most joy-filled of all. St. Francis de Sales said that "for those who live in the world and desire to live in true virtue, it is necessary to unite together in holy, sacred friendship."[36]

Our friendship with Jesus enables us to enjoy life-giving friendships that help us to grow in love and joy. The blessing of a true friend knows no bounds, as this pasasage from the Book of Sirach reminds us:

Faithful friends are a sturdy shelter;
    whoever finds one finds a treasure.
Faithful friends are beyond price,
    no amount can balance their worth.
Faithful friends are life-saving medicine;
    those who fear God will find them. (Sirach 6:14-16)

There are also special mentoring friendships, like the ones shared between St. Paul and Timothy or St. Francis de Sales and St. Jane de Chantal, or the one that we can imagine existed between the Blessed Mother and St. Mary Magdalene. In such friendships, initiated by the Holy Spirit, two souls are brought together; one has the ability to see a little bit further down the road of faith to act as a guide for the other. The bond of these friendships is usually lifelong and transcends any physical distance between the two.

If you are someone who has trouble making friends or trusting others, ask the Lord to heal those wounds so that you can embrace the joy of godly friendships. Jesus chose his friends carefully, and we are called to do the same. We are advised to "let those who are friendly to you be many, / but one in a thousand [be] your confidant" (Sirach 6:6). I believe that when we pray for Jesus to send us godly friends, he always provides. He knows how important good friendships are and how necessary they are for our souls.

Lord, please connect me with faithful friends.

Joy Note: Are you a faithful friend?

Unconditional Joy

I keep the LORD always before me;
with him at my right hand, I shall never be shaken.
Therefore my heart is glad, my soul rejoices.

—PSALM 16:8-9

If you are looking for a worthy spiritual goal, let it be to experience unconditional joy, a joy that transcends and covers all, a joy that scales the heights and plumbs the depths and remains steadfast and true. Unconditional joy is a supernatural gift given out of love for the purpose of love. It is available to you, but you have to believe that it is possible.

We can't conjure up joy on our own power, but we can live with our arms wide open to receive it. Here are some words from St. Catherine of Siena, translated into everyday language, that we can put into practice:

Be happy, be content—always everywhere in all circumstances—because every circumstance is a gift from your eternal Father. That's why God wants us to rejoice in every one of our troubles and to praise and give glory to his name—yes, in everything because God loves you with a forever kind of love. Buck up! Remember who loves you, and be encouraged today and everyday in Christ, gentle Jesus.[36]

God loves us with a forever kind of love, and his love gives us the courage and strength to cast off our cloaks of negativity and pick up a new pair of glasses. With these new "lenses," we can see the ever-present potentiality of joy in all circumstances. This is the will of God for us in Christ Jesus (1 Thessalonians 5:18). In the verse that follows, we are directed, "Do not quench the Spirit" (5:19). The Holy Spirit is a spirit of joy. When he possesses us and we possess him, the outcome can be nothing but joy.

Joy is the living water of our souls, replenished by the nourishment of Jesus when we receive his Body and Blood. Jesus offered his life as a sacrifice for our joy, and we offer him the greatest thanks when we live lives of unconditional joy.

Dear Lord, help me to "buck up" and be joyful, no matter what happens!

Joy Note: Do you believe in unconditional joy?

Hope and Joy

*May the God of hope fill you with all joy
and peace in believing.*

—ROMANS 15:13

Hope and joy are beautifully entwined; they are the silver and gold strands of the spiritual life. Hope begets joy, and joy begets hope—it's a partnership of virtues worth pursuing. Hope and joy are the lifelines of the soul, pulling us out of the mire of our mistakes and into the safe haven of God's merciful and loving heart.

Hope and joy are the fuel that keeps the fire in our souls burning; the breath of the Holy Spirit fans the flames. Without hope and joy, we cannot live, and we cannot love completely. God speaks to us through the words of Jeremiah when he says:

For I know well the plans I have in mind for you . . . plans for your welfare and not for woe, so as to give you a future of hope. When you call me, and come and pray to me, I will listen to you. When you look for me, you will find me. Yes, when you seek me with all your heart, I will let you find me . . . and I will change your lot. (Jeremiah 29:11-14)

God is saying that no matter where we have been or what we have done, our future is full of hope in him. He will turn our mourning into dancing (Psalm 30:12). He will take our present circumstances and change them into something good. He will listen and come near to us in our time of need. He will let himself be found (Jeremiah 29:13-14).

Whether they are the jewels in our crown or the nails in our cross, hope and joy are precious gifts from our loving Father. We simply need to surrender to his love and receive them. We surrender when we seek him with our whole heart, when we love him for his sake alone and leave everything in his hands.

Hope is the deep breath of the soul—the drawing in. Joy is the eternal exhaling, the evidence of a God who dwells within. Together they form a life of peace that cannot be denied.

May the God of hope fill you with joy—always.

Lord, let hope and joy fill my heart and rule my life.

Joy Note: How will you seek God with your whole heart?

Acknowledgments

Endnotes

1. Vincent Serpa, OP, taken from Catholic Answers website, Quick Questions, "How Does the Church Define Coveting?" Accessed at http://www.catholic.com/quickquestions/how-does-the-church-define-coveting.

2. Quoted in Steve Mueller, ed., *God With* Us (St. Louis: All Saints Press, 2013), 17.

3. Thérèse of Lisieux, *Story of a Soul,* tr. John Clarke, OCD (Washington, DC: ICS Publications, 1996), 194.

4. Barbershop Harmony Society website, "Health Benefits of Singing." Accessed at http://www.barbershop.org/index.php/about/sing/competitions/past-champions/youth-zone/history/preservation/news-a-events-main/291-health-benefits-of-singing.html.

5. Benedict XVI, Homily at Chrism Mass, Holy Thursday, 2010.

6. Search Quotes Website. Accessed at http://www.search-quotes.com/quotation/ An_infinite_God_can_give_all_of_Himself_to_each_of_His_children._He_does_not_distribute_Himself_that/362683/

7. Father George W. Kosicki, CSB, *Rejoice in the Lord Always!* (Steubenville, Ohio: Franciscan University Press, 1993), 3, 4.

8. Kosicki, *Rejoice in the Lord Always!*, 4.

9. *St. Thérèse of Lisieux, Last Conversations*, translated by John Clarke, OCD (Washington, DC: ICS Publications, 1977), 261.

10. *The Collected Works of St. Teresa of Ávila*, vol. 2, translated by Kiernan Kavanaugh, OCD, and Otilio Roriguez, OCD (Wahington, DC: ICS Publications, 2012), 39.

11. Thomas à Kempis, *The Imitation of Christ*, translated by Aloysius Croft and Harold Bolton (Mineola, NY: Dover Publications, 2003), 23.

12. EWTN website, accessed at http://www.ewtn.com/faith/edith_stein.htm.

13. Waltraud Herbstrith, *Edith Stein: A Biography* (San Francisco: Ignatius, 1992), 185, 187.

14. William Shakespeare, *Troilus and Cressida,* act 1, scene 2.

15. St. Thérèse of Lisieux, *Last Conversations*, 57.

16. Sergio Rubin and Francesca Ambrogetti, *Pope Francis: Conversations with Jorge Bergoglio: His Life in His Own Words* (New York: Putnam, 2013).

17. Quoted in Wayne Muller, *Legacy of the Heart: The Spiritual Advantages of a Painful Childhood* (New York: Simon and Schuster, 1992), 92.

18. Fulton J. Sheen, *Treasure in Clay: The Autobiography of Fulton J. Sheen* (New York: Random House, 2009), 202.

19. Robert J. Wicks, *Snow Falling on Snow* (New York: Paulist Press, 2001), 100.

20. Raymond Arroyo, *Mother Angelica's Little Book of Life Lessons and Everyday Spirituality* (New York: Doubleday, 2007), 183.

21. Ibid., 186.

22. "Pope: Confession is the place to experience mercy, grace." Catholic News Service, April 2, 2013. http://www.catholicnews.com/data/stories/cns/1301483.htm.

23. Pope Francis, Twitter post, June 30, 2013.

24. Paraphrased by Pope John Paul II from Letter 368, Closing Homily for World Youth Day, August 20, 2000. The actual quote is "If you are what you ought to be, you will set fire to all Italy."

25. "Pope at Mass: Christian joy far from simple fun," May 10, 2013. News.Va, accessed at http://www.news.va/en/news/pope-at-mass-christian-joy-far-from-simple-fun.

26. Fulton J. Sheen, *YOU* (Hebron, Kentucky: Beacon Publishing, 2013), 14.

27. "What Is Lectio Divina?" Taken from Order of the Carmelites website, Order of the Brothers of Blessed Virgin Mary of Mount Carmel, accessed at http://ocarm.org/en/content/lectio/what-lectio-divina.

28. *Alcoholics Anonymous: The Big Book*, 4th edition, (AA World Services: New York, 2001), 562.

29. Cathy Morris, "Finding Spiritual Balance." Taken from "Lovest Thou Me" website, accessed at http://lovestthoume.com/FeedMySheep/FindingSpiritualBalance.html.

30. Teresa of Ávila, *Interior Castle*, II, 9.

31. "Heaven." In The Catholic Encyclopedia. New York: Robert Appleton Company. Retrieved from New Advent website: http://www.newadvent.org/cathen/07170a.htm.

32. Brian Kolodiejchuk, MC, *Mother Teresa: Come Be My Light* (New York: Doubleday, 2007), 227.

33. Carmen Acevedo Butcher, *Incandescence: 365 Readings with Woman Mystics* (Brewster, MA: Paraclete Press, 2005), 186.

34. David Steindl Rast, "Recollections of Thomas Merton's Last Days in the West," *Monastic Studies,* vol. 7, 1, 10.

35. Francis de Sales, *Introduction to the Devout Life* (Rockford, IL: Tan Books and Publishers, 1994), 174.

36. Carmen Acevedo Butcher, *Incandescence: 365 Readings with Woman Mystics*, 15.

Journaling Space

_____

_____

_____

_____

_____

_____

_____

_____

_____

_____

_____

_____

_____

_____

_____

the WORD
among us®
The *Spirit* of Catholic Living

This book was published by The Word Among Us. Since 1981, The Word Among Us has been answering the call of the Second Vatican Council to help Catholic laypeople encounter Christ in the Scriptures.

The name of our company comes from the prologue to the Gospel of John and reflects the vision and purpose of all of our publications: to be an instrument of the Spirit, whose desire is to manifest Jesus' presence in and to the children of God. In this way, we hope to contribute to the Church's ongoing mission of proclaiming the gospel to the world so that all people would know the love and mercy of our Lord and grow ever more deeply in love with him.

Our monthly devotional magazine, *The Word Among Us*, features meditations on the daily and Sunday Mass readings, and currently reaches more than one million Catholics in North America and another half million Catholics in one hundred countries around the world. Our book division, The Word Among Us Press, publishes numerous books, Bible studies, and pamphlets that help Catholics grow in their faith.

To learn more about who we are and what we publish, log on to our website at www.wau.org. There you will find a variety of Catholic resources that will help you grow in your faith.

Embrace His Word, Listen to God . . .

www.wau.org